To Ellen

— Megen Clark

I TIED MY SHOES TODAY

Recovering from a Hemorrhagic Stroke

MEGON PHILLIPS AESCH

Archway Publishing books may be ordered
through booksellers or by contacting:

Archway Publishing
1663 Liberty Drive
Bloomington, IN 47403
www.archwaypublishing.com
1 (888) 242-5904

Because of the dynamic nature of the Internet, any web addresses or
links contained in this book may have changed since publication and
may no longer be valid. The views expressed in this work are solely those
of the author and do not necessarily reflect the views of the publisher,
and the publisher hereby disclaims any responsibility for them.

Any people depicted in stock imagery provided by Thinkstock are
models, and such images are being used for illustrative purposes only.
Certain stock imagery © Thinkstock.

ISBN: 978-1-4808-3654-9 (sc)
ISBN: 978-1-4808-3655-6 (e)

Library of Congress Control Number: 2016914347

Print information available on the last page.

Archway Publishing rev. date: 10/25/2016

Dedication

For everyone, but especially for Mom and Dad and for Jim.

(Sung by Celine Dion. Lyrics and music by Diane Warren.)

You were my strength when I was weak

You were my voice when I couldn't speak

You were my eyes when I couldn't see

You were the best there was in me

Lifted me up when I couldn't reach

You gave me faith 'coz you believed

I'm everything I am

Because you loved me

Acknowledgments

Thank you, Jim, for taking our marriage vows so seriously and for more than I can ever thank you for. It has been a long, difficult road, and I thank you for not only believing that I would survive, but could recover.

Mom, thank you so much for everything. For the laundry you did, the beds you made, the meals you cooked, the miles you drove to therapy, and even for feeding the dogs!

Thank you, Dad, for all of those trips to Ballston Spa. I still think we could handle three ice cream cones! (I *did* notice that was the only time we went to therapy alone!)

Thank you Mike, for your "behind the scenes" help. Thanks, too, for introducing us to Dr. Jenkyn!

Dr. Jenkyn, thank you for answering my many questions, for writing the eloquent forward and for taking my case, in the first place. It truly is because of you, that this has been written. I thank you for that and for treating my entire family with the dignity they deserved.

To Helen without whom this book would really not have been at all possible. Saying "Thank you" isn't enough.

Forward

Medical Record Note: Megon Aesch, 23 August
Problem List:
Cerebellar AVM
SP/VP Shunt
S/ No New Symptoms
O/ Going Home 9-4
A/ Miracle
P/ RTC prn (return to clinic as needed)

With this entry into her medical chart, my
tenure of neurological care for Megon Aesch ended
(or so I thought). My office "SOAP" (Subjective/
Objective/Assessment/Plan) note from that August
day reflected, in one word, the achievement of this
remarkable individual in her monumental struggle
back from coma and persistent vegetative state to
life again at home. Miracle, period.

I first came to know Megon on 4 January,
when she was transferred to my care six months

after her brain hemorrhage. It was through the determined efforts of her neurosurgeon and her Neurology Ward Team, the ministrations of the dedicated caregivers in our hospital including the Neuroscience Nursing Staff, the Social Services Staff, and the many Physical and Occupational Therapists of the Dartmouth-Hitchcock Medical Center in Lebanon, New Hampshire, that Megon began her long journey of recovery. This journey would take Megon to the Greenery in Boston, Massachusetts and Wesley Health Care in Saratoga Springs, New York, before returning her to her home in Cambridge, New York.

The unflagging devotion of her husband, Jim, her parents, Gail and Ed, and her brother, Mike, are chronicled here in her memoir. The support of her extended family, her Physical Therapists and friends, Tammi ("she never gave up on me!") and Judy ("she convinced me to work hard without my ever realizing what I was doing.") and her rehabilitation supporter and co-patient, Glen ("my 'cheerleader' at Wesley"), among others underscore what caring humans can and will do for each other.

Megon lost her memory for close to two years of her life. Jim provides us with insight into this lost time with his recount of Megon's day-to-day medical problems, which render her unaware, probably blessedly so, of those circumstances. Fragments of those memories would only later be recovered, as Megon put it, "when the penny dropped."

Megon describes her first walk on a South Carolina beach, the pungent smell of moist potting soil in her horticulture class, and the arduous process of relearning to talk and swallow as landmarks in her recovery. Her need to be with others ("I just did not want to be alone.") and the support she needed most from her caregivers and loved ones ("the most important thing that I can think of would be encouragement.") are also poignantly described here.

Megon's brother, Mike, wrote to me, "It is our belief now that, knowing Megon as we do, one day she will thank you herself.* From being a Rotary Exchange Student to Sweden, to graduating from Cornell University with highest honors, to starting, and very successfully running her own greenhouse operation! It has to be that spirit that is keeping her going through this nightmare. We are all praying that someday Meg will be able to show us some of that independence again, if it is physically possible, and she will do the rest!"

And she has. Read how the penny dropped for Megon Aesch.

*Megon did when she personally emailed me.

Lawrence R. Jenkyn, M.D.
Section of Neurology
Dartmouth-Hitchcock Medical Center
Lebanon, New Hampshire

Prologue

This is my story, but it cannot be told without my husband, my mother and father, and my brother. It is about love, growth, disaster and renewal. The story begins much earlier than the events recounted here.

I was born in potting soil! I helped my mom and grandmother with chores in their gardens as far back as I can remember: important chores like "running" and "fetching." When I was old enough to decide such things, I knew growing plants would be my life's work. From then on, I carefully "cultivated" my dream of owning my own greenhouse business.

During high school, I worked for a retail greenhouse, learning all that I could about growing and caring for plants, and about talking with customers. Loving every minute of it, I learned important things, like "the customer is always right!" (Within reason, of course). No matter what happened, we were always supposed to show that whatever our customer wanted was the right thing. I was exhausted every night, but it was a good kind of exhaustion -- just bone weary from hard physical work. I was doing what I loved, and knowing I was on my way to college, I was also very happy.

I was accepted at Cornell University and graduated high school, but I deferred attendance to Cornell to realize another dream. I spent a year in Sweden as an exchange student, living with a family that became very dear to me.

I went to Cornell, and I received a bonus while standing in line at registration. I heard someone call my name and turned around to find Jim, a friend from home whom I hadn't seen for a while. Jim, as it turned out, was starting his senior year as an Environmental Science Major. The renewed friendship soon became romance. Here was a guy who loved the outdoors as much as I did: Someone with whom I could share my goals and dreams.

Four years later, I earned a B.S. in horticulture, returned home and worked a couple of greenhouse management jobs while saving toward my life goal of owning my own greenhouse business.

Jim and I married, and the following year we found and purchased an old farmhouse in a little town in upstate New York, not far from my hometown. Our new home needed work, but it had a lot of "character" and plenty of land to grow my future business. We immediately began renovating the house and cleaning up the property in anticipation of the greenhouses we would construct there.

We built the first greenhouse and started a wholesale operation. I grew pack annuals and geraniums for spring sales along with hanging baskets and other assorted plants. In the fall, I sold chrysanthemums and ornamental cabbage and kale.

As part of my business, I sold and took care of plants in Manchester, Vermont. I used to run up and down stairs onto the decks of condominiums to work on the plants. I had so much energy then!

Although Jim kept his other job, together we worked on building the greenhouse business, developing a customer base, and expanding our greenhouse growing area over the next few years. The second year, we added our second greenhouse, and the following year, we added the third.

The first sign that all was not well came that fall. My usual stamina eluded me. I was concerned, but I thought I was tired because I had had such a busy summer. I had tingling in my arms and my hands, and occasionally my arms fell asleep at night. I still remember waking up one morning and being startled to find a hand in my face. When I realized it was my own hand, I shook it awake and laughed off my little scare, convincing myself that what I was experiencing wasn't really unusual. It could simply be explained by overuse in my greenhouse business. Jim was tired, too, making it seem more believable.

We decided to take a break and planned a vacation in Ireland. We had visions of castles, rock-walled green fields with sheep in them, warm woolen sweaters...and rain. Before the trip, I went to a doctor for a complete physical just to make sure nothing was wrong.

I told the doctor that I felt lethargic and not quite "up to par." He thought I wasn't displaying enough symptoms to warrant a CAT scan or an MRI, either of which might have indicated my problem. Because of my work, I also thought that perhaps I had contracted Lyme disease. My doctor thought that was a possibility, also. He ordered blood tests, and they, came back negative.

A good vacation seemed like the right "cure," so we focused on our upcoming trip to Ireland. The plan was, basically, to have no plan. We both followed such rigorous schedules that we wanted to experience life without a strict schedule for a while. We rented a car and set out from Shannon

Airport, driving from one guest home to the next. We had a reservation at just the first Bed and Breakfast where we planned to stay. After that, we met people who made suggestions, or we would stop at a pub and get recommendations for a place to sleep. Occasionally, the pub owner called ahead for us, or sometimes the proprietor even owned the B & B and we would be given reservations.

This vacation was just what we needed. No telephones ringing for me and no odd jobs that demanded Jim's attention. We roamed the countryside, visited castles, and hung out with the locals for two weeks.

Jim's favorite remembrance about our trip is when we quizzed the elderly owner of the Bed and Breakfast where we stayed in Doolin about which pub he would go to for dinner, he said, "There's only two pubs in town, and I go to both!" We were never quite certain if he was being diplomatic, or if he did, in fact, like both places equally. At any rate, the one we chose had great food, great beer, and great music, and was certainly a great time.

Difficult as it was to leave, we returned home with renewed vigor and enthusiasm. I thought my health problems were behind me.

We jumped into the following year with our minds racing ahead to the future. Life was good.

I was a 34-year-old career-oriented horticulturist with a good business and a great husband. Jim and I had dreams, goals and focus. We had a plan, and then we had disaster. We were hit with a blow beyond imagination.

On July 9th, several months after we travelled to Ireland, I had a stroke caused by an arteriovenous malformation: an AVM. Less than one per cent of the population has a brain AVM.[1] Clots producing blockages in blood vessels cause most strokes. Mine occurred when a deformed linkage between an artery and a vein burst causing excess blood to pool and exert pressure on my brain. I had a neurological AVM. A brain AVM.

Normally, arteries carry oxygen-rich blood from the heart to the brain where it enters a network of tiny capillaries. In most people, the capillaries cause a gradual flow from arteries to veins. An AVM lacks the effects of capillaries, which usually supply oxygen and nutrients to cells and pick up carbon dioxide and waste. In an AVM, the high-pressure arteries and the low-pressure veins are directly joined without having a capillary bed between them, causing

---

[1] http://www.floridahospital.com/arteriovenous-malformation-avm/statistics

the connection to burst. This is what led to my severe headache and stroke.

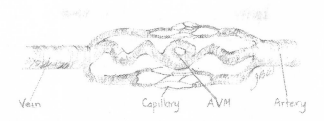

AVMs are defects of the circulatory system probably arising during fetal development or right after birth. They are congenital, but not hereditary. AVMs can occur anywhere in the body, although common sites include the lungs, kidney, liver, brain, brainstem and spinal cord. Those located in the brain are quite damaging. In my case, the AVM was located in the cerebellum area of my brain. It *did* burst.

People with neurological AVMs sometimes experience few, if any, symptoms. They simply go through life with it causing no problems. In such cases, the AVM is noticed only during treatment for an unrelated illness or during autopsy. About eighty-eight per cent of those with an AVM are asymptomatic.[2] The headaches I was having, may or may not have been indicative of an AVM. A doctor once told my parents that the AVM was like a "birthmark" -- something that was just with me, lying dormant, until that particular day, when it burst.

When I first became aware, one year and eight months after the AVM, I could not understand why I couldn't perform even the simplest routine tasks. Brushing my hair or teeth were both difficult tasks for me. My hands would not move the way I thought they should be moving.

My doctors told Jim that the cerebellum is the area of the brain most responsible for balance and coordination. It is located at the back of the brain. I have a "dent" in my head at the sight where my doctors removed some of the skull to relieve the excess pressure on my brain and to attain better access to the AVM. I had to remember to tell my hairstylist about the dent, so she would not become alarmed!

The cerebellum maintains posture by sensing where the limbs are. I can still hear one of my physical therapists say "posture" (pronouncing it "pos-cha") when I did exercises. I was supposed to

---

[2] http://www.floridahospital.com/arteriovenous-malformation-avm/statistics

always be thinking about where I was and what my limbs were doing. They help me attain some balance and stability.

The trauma my body has endured -- and my family has endured as well -- has been considered insurmountable. Some doctors told my husband and parents that I would never recover. Others told them I would never breathe without assistance, would never "lose" the trach, would never speak, would never feed myself, and a myriad of other "nevers." There was to be a long struggle ahead.

Years after having the AVM, I'm still sitting in a wheelchair because my balance is not good. I *am strong*, but my balance is bad. I am still having some difficulty speaking, although my mother will tell you that doesn't stop me from talking! My eyesight is also a problem. My acuity is only corrected to 20/60. Therefore, I quite often have difficulty understanding people. (I believe that we read lips more than we realize).

When we lose the benefit of having good eyesight, our ability to hear and understand is also impaired. However, I still work at improving. Jim has often told me that if I don't continue to work at making changes, I won't get better.

My physical therapists tell me, and I *have* to believe it, that every time I stand up, it accomplishes something. It is important to just get out of the wheelchair. Sometimes, I try to sit up really straight on the floor, engaging the muscles along my torso. Another good exercise is to stand with my back against the wall for support. These things help, because my brain is still trying to remember how to balance.

This experience has taught me that the mind is much more powerful (even when damaged) than most of us will ever know. The ember burning deep within each of us that drives us to succeed, to be optimistic, even to survive... all generated from a collection of nerve cells and blood vessels. I cannot help but think that there must be so much more to it than that. Where does emotion come from? Resolve and determination? I don't have any answers, but I do know that inspiration and positive thinking are contagious. Thank you to everyone who believed in me and helped me. All of you have worked so hard, and it has all been worthwhile.... to me.

"Whether you think you can or you think you can't -- you're right".

--Henry Ford--

Chapter 1
Ithaca

In the months between our trip to Ireland and the day the AVM finally exploded, we lived at our normal hectic pace. Jim worked his regular job, and together we worked on running the greenhouse business.

Looking back, my only real problem had occurred in June, about two weeks prior to the time my AVM erupted. My brother, Mike, and I were preparing a nice dinner for our parents' 39th wedding anniversary. (I still remember we were making prime rib of beef.) While we were preparing the meal, my neck became so stiff and sore that I asked Jim to massage it for me.

The doctors later told my parents that the sore neck could have been a symptom of the AVM, but I blamed it on too much work. My hands were also falling asleep. Despite wearing a brace at night, I would wake up alarmed that there was no feeling in my arm and hand. This, too, I blamed on my work.

Had I experienced other symptoms (such as a severe headache) earlier, I might have had an MRI or CAT scan, and the problem may have been diagnosed before any real damage was done. As it turned out, on July 9, (when the terrible headache occurred), things rapidly spiraled out of my control.

On that day, I was in Ithaca, New York with Linda, my friend and fellow horticulturist. We had attended a plant conference at my alma mater, Cornell University.

When the notice arrived in the mail about the bedding plant conference, it seemed to be perfect for our situation. Jim and I were happy that our greenhouse business was growing so quickly, but at the same time, we had some difficult decisions to make. Should we remain as a wholesale business? This would mean buying a large parcel of land so we could erect more greenhouses to grow more plants. We had also discussed limiting our business size by going retail. If so, we would buy a smaller piece of land and construct a store there.

In the case of remaining wholesale and expanding while staying efficient, I would have to learn to be less of a perfectionist and become more production oriented. I also considered doing some specialty growing, which would entail starting specific plants for other growers whom I hoped to meet at the conference. I wanted to make some contacts and find out what others were looking for. Was there one specific crop that I could grow very well for others?

In addition to finding some of the answers to my questions, it would be a treat to return to the Cornell campus and experience life there without worrying about the next bio exam. Added to that, I was happy to have the opportunity to stay with Lee, a good friend from our college days.

Cornell University is located in Ithaca, a beautiful town in the Finger Lakes Region of upstate New York. Ithaca is most known for its colleges and the hills they inhabit. Cornell sits on East Hill, with Cayuga Lake and the town sprawled down below it. College Town, with its apartments, restaurants and bars, all of which cater to students, is halfway up the hill. Ithaca College sits across town on South Hill.

I remember parts of that weekend vividly. Linda and I had spent the long weekend attending seminars and taking tours. Braving the heat, we took a conference bus to visit local farms. On July eighth, it was nearly 100 degrees but it felt even warmer on the bus. I am told I had gotten some great ideas, but mostly I remember the farms.

At one grower's orchard, we were encouraged to eat all the cherries we could. We picked them off the trees and ate quite a few in an effort to cool down. We were all pretty parched, and the juice from the cherries helped. They were a welcome treat on such a hot day.

The next day, July 9, Linda and I were scheduled to leave Ithaca. Happy, full of fresh ideas, and wanting to enjoy our last day there to its fullest, Linda and I decided to attend the farmers' market in downtown Ithaca, before we started the 4-hour journey home.

The building that houses the market is a big, fresh-air pavilion looking out on Cayuga Lake. The views of the lake were beautiful. It was breathtaking, and I remember thinking this farmers' market was nicer than any I had ever been to.

I also remember that it was another really hot day. Just as Linda and I were readying to leave the Market, I got such a severe headache that I had to sit down. I looked at Linda and her lips were moving, but I couldn't hear any words. It felt as if there were explosions taking place in my head. I have never felt anything like it. My headache was so intense that I felt nauseated, but I remember thinking that it was the heat that made me feel sick to my stomach.

The pain in my head was excruciating. I finally understood what people meant when they said they had a "splitting" headache. I had never before experienced a migraine, but I thought my headache must be very much like one. It seemed like the din of the crowd was just too loud. I really wanted all the people to get quiet for a while. The sun seemed to be too hot and too bright.

I remember thinking that I just had to sit down for a minute or two so the headache would go away. Maybe it would at least subside enough so that I could function.

I told Linda I would meet her outside. I then went out, carrying my purchase of a bag of ripe cherries, and sat down to wait for Linda. The cherries were for my mother; they were a favorite of hers. I didn't know at the time that they would not be eaten. Instead, they were left there to rot. I sank down to the grass and I put my head down on my arms, trying to shield my eyes from the sun.

I could only imagine that people were likely all staring at me as I sat there on the grass and tried to collect myself. I was hoping no one would stop and ask if I was okay. I didn't know what my answer would be. The way I was feeling, I could not talk. I didn't want to. I didn't even want to look at anyone. I remember feeling a bit scared. I just *hurt*.

The idea of communicating with others slipped beyond my imagination. I couldn't even see. I had never experienced pain like that in my life.

I took some aspirin, and when I felt a little better (When I felt well enough to drive, anyway), we went back to get our suitcases from Lee's house. Looking back, I cannot believe I drove even that distance.

As we picked up our luggage and got into the car to drive home, my headache returned. It was stronger than it had ever been, and I remember turning to Linda and asking, "Do you drive a stick shift?" Those were the last words I remember speaking.

They were, in fact, the last words I would speak for 20 months, when I started "waking up" in Wesley Health Care Center in Saratoga Springs, New York, a rehabilitation center with one floor for young adults.

I understand that it is difficult to recognize an AVM and that I was lucky that I wasn't working when it happened, because I usually worked alone. I was also lucky that my friend immediately recognized the seriousness of my situation.

Being with Linda that day was the first of many fortunate events that occurred to make my recovery possible. I have since learned that Linda lost a friend to an AVM. She, therefore, knew what was happening to me. If it weren't for her quick thinking, things may have been much different.

Lee directed Linda to a clinic in Ithaca. Fortunately for me, when Linda started driving, she closed the windows and turned the air conditioning way up, probably slowing down my metabolism and thus slowing the bleed. She later told my father that it was like there was an angel sitting on her shoulder telling her what to do.

At the clinic, they were unable to treat me, because they had no neurological specialists. They sent me to a nearby hospital, but that hospital had no specialists either.

I was airlifted to University Hospital in Syracuse, New York, where there were specialists on duty. Our flight was delayed by a terrible thunderstorm. The pilot was uneasy about flying through the storm. The doctors at Syracuse said they should "just get her here as soon as possible." About three and a half hours elapsed from the time that the AVM ruptured until the time I was treated. It is possible that had I been treated faster, not as much damage would have occurred, although with the type of stroke I had, the damage probably occurred instantaneously.

My husband was at work in Saratoga Springs, New York, when he was notified of my situation. He was told that I was being treated at Syracuse University Hospital. He, in turn, phoned my parents who had been enjoying dinner at my aunt and uncle's house in Manchester, Vermont. My parents left for Syracuse immediately, stopping in Saratoga to pick Jim up. They all arrived at the hospital just minutes after I got out of the operating room.

I underwent three hours of emergency surgery to seal the arteries and stop the bleeding. I would undergo a second surgery to remove the AVM before I left that hospital to go to a rehabilitation facility in Rutland, Vermont, which was closer to home than Syracuse. My brother also lived nearby.

My husband kept a journal during the year and a half when I was simply not cognizant of what was happening around me. This has helped to fill in the blank spaces for me. I am so lucky and thankful that he kept that journal. It is the only way I could learn what happened during that time. During this period, I had stayed in three hospitals and four rehabilitation centers, although I don't remember any of them, except of course, the last one -- Wesley.

While I was extremely happy and thankful to read Jim's journal, I also became very depressed when I did, only because it discussed people and events that I could never know. It seemed odd that he was so familiar with those people. He talked about them like he knew them. How could he know those people so well when I didn't know them at all? What a strange feeling to lose those months of my life. It did bother me, pricking me as if with a pin. I had missed so much. How could I have been that ill?

Writing my diary and this book has brought to mind some things that have happened in the time that I was "sick". I was oblivious to much of what was going on around me at that point. Years later, I still have no memory of that time. My parents and my husband told me most of it. I really didn't remember anything until I began "waking up" that February, a year and eight months after I "fell asleep." What was termed "becoming aware" to me was "waking up!" I slowly became aware of people and things around me.

Even then, things seemed to not really be occurring. They were surreal -- dreamlike. I seemed to float along. I would be in my room, and then I would be in a therapy room on the first floor of my building. I didn't remember exactly how I got there. I couldn't even remember getting up and getting dressed in the morning.

When I "woke up," I remember looking at magazines and paying special attention to year-end issues to find out what had happened while I was unaware. I also remember being very interested in television specials like "The Tonies" and "The Grammies" to find out what music and shows had been popular during that time.

In general, the timing involved never seemed to make sense to me. I found myself continually asking, "I lived where? When?" The pieces didn't fit together right. To say that I was very confused doesn't begin to describe the feelings I had.

Jim finally drew up a time-line for me that helped quite a bit. It was in a page protector for safekeeping and I carried it gingerly, like my life depended on it, referring to it when I couldn't remember where I was or where I had lived at a certain time. Because of my confusion, I carried that time-line with me wherever I went.

I have had my "ups and downs," but through it all nobody in our family has given up on me. It is very important to have a lot of good support, as well as an advocate when you are unable to make your own decisions. I know that I didn't always show how much I appreciate everyone, especially when I'm frustrated!

This book is based on information my family, friends, doctors, nurses, and therapists have helped me piece together throughout my recovery. I have written about things I have slowly remembered, but I rely strongly on Jim's journal and refer to it frequently in the following chapters. I also included his journal as an appendix to this book, because without the journal the book could not have been written. Without Jim, my parents, my brother, and the rest of my family, I could not have come this far, and to them I will always be grateful.

Chapter 2

Syracuse

All that I know about what happened between that July when I got into the car at Lee's house and that February -- one year and eight months later, when I "woke up" in Wesley Health Care Center in Saratoga Springs, New York -- I learned from talking to my husband, my parents, my friend Linda, and others who lived through it with me. This is difficult for me to even fathom.

I never liked anyone telling me what to do and making decisions for me. Yet, with the onset of that terrible headache, I was transformed from a very strong-willed, active adult into a completely helpless patient. With few exceptions, I was no longer "Meg" to anyone except my family and friends, who loved and cared for me and prayed for my health and virtual survival.

In trying to piece it all together afterward, I asked everyone quite an array of questions. I was not always ready for the answers. In one of the first conversations I had with Linda and my mother after I returned home, I became very agitated and emotional. Like any patient with a serious condition, I could not accept it. I fought against it. I denied it. I was angry that it had happened against my will, and I was sad that it had.

When Jim gave me his journal, he did it to help me understand what had happened, to help me accept that it was real and to assimilate it. In a sense, he helped me take back my story: to take back my life.

When I read it, I grieved, not only for what had happened to me, but for what had happened to my family. It was staggering to learn how many times, in the grip of fear for my life, they had to make decisions for me and pray that they were the right ones.

My illness was not one sudden drop into an abyss and a slow, steady climb out. It was painful to learn that I would sometimes rally, raising their hopes, then plunge into a different kind of hell that left them struggling to cope.

The only relief Jim received came when he phoned in to work soon after I had the AVM.

His Human Resource representative told him that the Family and Medical Leave Act of 1993 (FMLA) assured him time off, and he shouldn't worry about the security of his job, but should, instead, "focus on Meg's needs."

In Syracuse, after my first critical phase, I actually was alert at different intervals. My father has informed me that one of my first doctors explained that it was important to always talk *to* me as if I was listening and not *around* me. Even with their attention, for the first two days after my surgery, I was not responsive.

On day three, when I opened my eyes for the first time, Jim wrote, "Those were the most beautiful eyes I'd ever seen. A miracle!" His exuberance was all too quickly tempered by CT scan results that showed blood and spinal fluid in the ventricles of my brain.

Still, when I greeted him the next day, he was "in heaven." The doctors told him I was beating the odds, but when they pulled my vent tube, I had to work too hard to breathe. They re-intubated me only one hour later. The roller coaster had begun.

Over the next few days, I seemed to make progress. They brought me music and I tapped my feet. I went on assisted walks up and down the hall, participated in therapy, and even showed off some of my Irish temper. One doctor, I am told, kept yelling at me as if I was deaf. (My hearing, if anything, became more acute during my ordeal as my vision grew worse.) On day six, he brought an entourage of medical students into my room, and with my family and nurses present, it was standing room only. Since I had a trachea tube in and couldn't speak audibly, he kept asking me to hold up two fingers to show that I heard him and understood him.

Evidently, he was so loud the people all over the hospital could hear him. I guess he annoyed me and I tried to ignore him. My family kept encouraging me to respond, so I did the only thing I could do to express my mischievous personality and dislike of the situation. You can guess which two fingers I held up. "ATTA GIRL!" Jim wrote in his journal.

The doctor made a quick exit. He didn't like it; didn't seem to find the humor in it. My family didn't have many reasons to laugh after that.

By day ten, I had been put on morphine because of a rough night, and an angiogram showed the location of the bleed. Jim and my parents were left with what Jim called "hard questions and decisions – should they operate or wait." There were risks on both sides. He called it a choice between "arsenic and cyanide." I wonder where he got his strength, and I wonder what I would have done in his place.

On day eleven, they extubated me again and I was coughing and swallowing with some success. By day twelve I was restless and anxious. Meanwhile, Jim was still trying to hold everything together. He went home to tend to my plants and forty people showed up to help! They had a chrysanthemum pinching party. (This was something I routinely did to encourage the best blooms.) Reading this, I was deeply touched that so many people would turn out to help my family and me.

At the same time, it was sobering to realize that events were racing ahead without my participation. Life did, in fact, go on. Jim and my parents had everyday tasks to struggle with, including the greenhouse business, while they tried to cope with my illness.

On day fourteen, I wrote my first letters in order to identify a plant for one of my nurses. I went for a supported walk with Jim on that same day, and he could feel that, although I still had strength, I had very little balance. My neurosurgeon told me about the new surgery they planned and Jim wrote, "I think she understood and agreed it was best. I think she trusts her doctor. Thank God." Learning that, at least this once, I had participated in a decision about my care and had – maybe – eased Jim's burden a little gave me some solace as I read on.

His words on day seventeen show what a deeply caring and loving man he is and how truly lucky I am that he was, and still is, here with me. He wrote, "She's incredibly strong and brave. I admire her for her courage. She's been so cooperative even though she's aware of the pain and discomfort." How brave did he and the rest of my family have to be to take a back seat and watch someone else make all of the decisions?

Once again, the words in his journal revealed what I fear was a painful time. "The throat suction was especially torturous for all of us, but she endures it without resistance." Realizing only a little of what *they* endured makes me feel guilty even though there was nothing I could do to prevent it. Unjustified as it is, that guilt sticks to me like an unwanted guest.

On day twenty, I was moved out of ICU and my family worried that I wasn't getting enough attention. Jim thought I was depressed and easily agitated. "I don't think they know her abilities," he wrote. "She has to be restrained to protect her." He knew I was, "frustrated with no communication ability."

That day, the doctors put in a percutaneous endoscopic gastrostomy (PEG) tube--or a tube inserted into my stomach for feeding. That way, I could be fed "more regularly and get stronger."

On the 22nd day, Jim thought, "Meg looks great today. Lots of visitors cheered her up." He also noted that I displayed "full range of emotion -- laughed, cried, even joked. I was working with her neck exercises and when she got tired, she strangled me! Enough with the neck!"

The very first surgery that I had was the surgery to quickly stop the brain bleed. The surgery to remove the AVM was delayed several days. (Someone else was scheduled before me. I suppose that means that someone else needed attention more than I did.) During that time, Jim noted every point of hope -- every time I walked, laughed, joked or worked hard in therapy. He took me outside for a stroll and wrote that I "didn't want the wheelchair to stop." He also worried over every misstep. I was mixing up my days and nights, and by day twenty-five, the day of our stroll, he was concerned that I was tired.

He and my family must have been exhausted by that time.

The surgery, to remove the AVM on August 4 (day twenty-seven) didn't go as planned – at least not for my family. They anxiously waited for over ten hours during a surgery that should have taken much less time, or so they thought. "I guess we were misinformed," Jim wrote. When the doctor and nurse finally emerged from the operating room, he said, they "looked totaled." The doctor told my family everything went "as expected." They said they "had some trouble controlling the bleeding, which increased the time."

My family finally left the hospital at 1:30 a.m., as I still had Recovery and a CT scan left. Jim said they were "semi-relieved." I presume they were pretty "wiped out" as well. I spent the next few days in relative quiet, recovering while my husband and parents continued their vigil.

They tried to keep me quiet the day after the surgery, according to Jim. A CT scan showed "ventricular swelling and blood in the ventricles. Had to add ventriculostomy line," Jim added.

On Day twenty-nine, he wrote, "She looks a little better today. Some swelling has gone down. She moves more easily and responds quicker. Still has pain and not too comfortable. Still, she is progressing as expected."

On the next day, he added "A better day overall. Swelling reduced. Eyes are nearly level now. Moves quite easily. Still has some pain. Kind of an up and down day. Alert and trying to talk at times. Moves extremities well."

On that day, he also noted that I had a "busy day," but that I "handled it well" with "lots of visitors."

By day thirty-six, I was "getting stronger and walking (assisted) more easily," but I was still restless at night. Jim thought I slept better when they were there. I fell out of bed that night at 11:00 p.m. Jim was told there were no injuries, but after that, he arranged to stay with me after hours.

On Jim's first night with me, I slept well and he had hoped that I would get my days and nights back "on track." The next day, number thirty-seven, my friend, Marcia visited, but Jim wrote that I "wasn't real responsive." This upsets me greatly to read, since Marcia was my best friend at college, and it means so much to me that she would visit me and my entire family.

I did sleep well again that night, but I was agitated the next day. Jim thought it was a reaction to Marcia leaving, but I also had a chest A-line removed, and there was discussion of my moving to another facility as well. There clearly was upheaval in my situation.

Actually, the move had been afoot for a while, as Jim and my parents had been working on it. The new place was a rehabilitation facility in Rutland, Vermont, where I was expected to have more physical and occupational therapy with an eye toward going home. There was a problem with the paperwork, however, and the move had been postponed.

Over the next few days, things went decidedly downhill. On day thirty-nine, Jim wrote that I was "withdrawn," and that it was "not a good day. Meg had a tough, restless night…me, too." Those last two little words pained my heart. Jim had always been there for me and I had been "restless."

On day forty-one, he noted only that the move to Rutland would be on Monday, but day forty-two was brighter. He happily noted that when my throat was checked my vocal chords were normal; I did "great" on a barium swallow test when my larynx closed "nearly all the way." I used an un-wheeled walker in physical therapy. He was truly excited for me, but over the next two days, we plunged into a new abyss.

On day forty-three, he wrote, "A very restless day followed by a pain in the neck night. Nurses are scarce and snotty. I'm wrestling non-stop with Meg and I'm exhausted...I've had as much as I can stand and I'm getting nasty." Day forty-four was even darker. Jim and my parents were unraveling at the seams as they watched me go through some new torture I couldn't convey. Jim poured his fear and anguish into his journal: "Meg is still agitated: squirming and wrestling with us. It's like watching an infant in a playpen full of broken glass. The tension of being on edge all the time is making us crazy. Meg got heavy sedatives tonight and she's still fighting and fidgeting two hours later." I read these words distressed for all of us. How did Jim and my parents survive a period that must have been torturous? What was happening to me then?

Still, on day forty-five they rallied as they moved me to Rutland. My father told me that, when they checked out of the hotel in Syracuse that they referred to as "home," they were told someone had paid for three nights' stay. It was such benevolence that made this time almost tolerable for them.

"Great things are ahead!" Jim wrote, willing himself and me forward, but I had another restless night after we arrived in Rutland. Jim thought I was nervous about the new surroundings. He had had no sleep in four days and left at 11:00 p.m. that night, hoping for the best. I wish I could have given it to him.

Chapter 3
Rutland

During the first eight days I spent in Rutland, Jim wrote only one journal entry. He thought that "the life-threatening medical stuff" was behind us, but it was more than that. The excitement he had tried to create over "great things ahead" slowly slipped from his grasp as days and nights blurred together with no improvement in my condition. The depths of his despair are perceptible in his words:

"Our expectations seem a bit high right now. We thought or hoped she would show rapid initial progress once in rehab, but it's not happening. Meg is still agitated and restless. She requires twenty-four-hour watch. She's quite capable of hurting herself and the nursing staff can't handle her needs. So Ed and Gail [Meg's parents] take turns during the day shifts and I cover the nights. Nights are absolute hell. You don't have the benefit of visitors and therapists to break up the monotony for you and you see Meg at her worst. She's either sleeping or agitated and lately she's been very restless. In a twelve-hour shift, she sleeps about four hours." It was as if I was trying to get away from the pressure building in my brain.

"I'm incredibly lonely," he continues. "There's no one to talk to. No one to get things off my chest to. I feel so trapped and alone. As for Meg's progress…it's hard to say. I don't see the therapy sessions and get only sketchy reports. They tell me things are improving…she's walking a little better; she's working on ADL's [Activities of Daily Living] and is quite good at dressing and brushing her teeth. She had a few spoons of food this week including chocolate pudding."

I lay awake at night sometimes now thinking about the pain and loneliness Jim suffered then and wish I could take it away. It's still in his voice when I ask him about my illness, so I try not to press it, but there is still so much I am struggling to understand. I have *so* many questions.

Jim's incredible resilience through it all still startles me. As low as he felt, he bounced right back at the slightest sign of any progress from me.

In the same journal entry that he wrote of being discouraged and lonely, he found reasons to hope. It seems like he couldn't bring himself to write of the negative without first finding something positive to add to it. It wasn't until August 31 that he found it.

"Today is a special day (August 31). They blocked her trach for one hour and the oximetry was great (97%). During that time, they also had her try to talk. What were her first words? 'Hi, mom,' of course."

He also noted on that day that we would have our first family meeting since arriving in Rutland, and thought they would "have a much better idea of where we're going after that." In his next entry, he said I had a "much more productive week," adding that I was "walking much better, still supported," and I had "much more control" with my right leg. Even the staff was encouraged by my progress.

He also made mention that I had a urinary infection. It would be all too soon apparent that infections such as this were as much a threat to me as my AVM, since high fevers would usually accompany them. This, however, was the least of my immediate problems.

On September 10, they pulled my trach tube, and Jim commented that I had had a good day and was responding well. He also said I was "very alert." I was even saying a few words, giving unsolicited hugs, and with support walking outside again.

The next day, I "did a 180." My head was hanging. I was slow to respond and "unwilling to do much." My therapists noticed a big difference in my ability to focus. Adding to that, Jim said my "agitation level had increased." They worried that pulling the trach had caused it, but my blood oxygen levels appeared normal.

The "backslide" continued and worsened as the week wore on. Finally, on September 16, using a CAT scan and comparison to my records that had just arrived from Syracuse, my neurosurgeon concluded that I had excessive fluid on my brain and drained it with a syringe.

Jim noticed an immediate difference, but, then over the weekend, I "continued to decline, becoming totally unresponsive by Sunday." I was conscious, but Jim wrote, "That's about all." Reading this, I felt that I was taking yet another turn on a roller coaster that wouldn't stop, and it was spinning more and more out of control.

The doctors put a ventriculo-peritoneal shunt (a tube running from the ventricles of the brain to the stomach cavity to relieve pressure on the brain) in my brain on Tuesday, September 20 [Day 74], and Jim prayed that this was "THE turning point." There had been so many false hopes before. After the shunt was added, Jim said my eyes were clearer, but I continued to act agitated, nauseous and unresponsive. The doctor told him that the "release of pressure can sometimes be as disruptive as the build-up."

In the midst of all this, because my progress wasn't quick enough, my insurance company said I would have to be re-located to a long-term care facility. Jim said, "I guess there are legal definitions of acute vs. long-term and Meg's progress is long-term." The discharge planner gave Jim an outdated five-year-old guide and told him to "find a place." After what Jim called "the family meeting from hell," they chose a place from "a very short list that didn't leave much choice."

Jim thought that it "almost seemed like she was listening," because soon after, I started responding again. I seemed to be much more willing to work in therapy. I interacted with visitors, followed motion, squeezed hands and gave them "pretty good thumbs up." It was as if I was trying to show them that I *could* stay in Rutland where my brother and his family lived.

During this time in Rutland, my niece Emma would offer me some company by climbing onto my hospital bed and drawing pictures of her horse and her dog. It must have been so comforting for me to see a familiar face during what, I am sure, was a very confusing time.

On day 96, October 10, I was relocated to a place called Hilltop, located in Niskayuna, New York. I have no memory of the place. After reading what my life was like there, I wish Jim and my parents didn't remember either.

My first twelve hours at that rehab were spent in a holding pattern while we waited to see a physician. No feeding, no catheterization, no explanations. Years later, my mother still can't talk about it without getting sad and angry. Dad mostly gets angry about the lack of a decent health care system in our "nation of assholes."

"When we arrived," Jim wrote, "it was sheer chaos…a damn zoo. I felt pretty sick and sad to think that Meg had to spend time here. It was just not as I remembered it [from my pre-admission visit].

"Therapists didn't show and the bed was a tiny, pathetic thing that she was beating herself

up in." Things didn't get any better the next day.
I was ready for therapy twice, but no one showed
up to get me there. The doctor ordered one-on-
one nursing for me between 3:00 p.m. and 7:00
a.m., so Jim could go home and get some rest. The
next day, Jim talked to Karen, my "sitter", who
told him I was "alert and responsive and seemed
to be accepting the move quite well."

How, then, did I have a grand mal seizure at
7:00 p.m. just after Jim arrived? "She stiffened up
and stopped breathing in my arms," Jim reported
in his journal. "I can't believe how calm I stayed
even though panic seemed to set in with the sitter.
They gave Meg oxygen and suctioned at first, then
medication. After a couple hours, she fell asleep,
so I left."

I had another seizure at 3:00 a.m. Jim left
home to go to work at 5:00 a.m. and wasn't told
about the seizure until he called at 8:30 a.m. No
doctor saw me until 9:00 a.m. How long would I
have waited if Jim hadn't called? The doctor sent
me to the hospital for tests.

About this experience with the hospital,
Jim wrote, "What a fiasco -- 12 hours in ER
and nobody was doing anything or taking
responsibility. We are lost, confused and no one
is telling us a damn thing." I could only imagine

his -- and my parents' -- torment. Reading Jim's words, I came to understand the raw emotion that would seize my family's faces when I asked about this period of time: gut-wrenching terror is how Jim described it.

I was finally admitted to the hospital at 8:00 that evening, October 13. The swelling in my head was back, but tests showed my ventricles were normal. Over the next few days, I became inactive. The doctors said my hydrocephalus was back and thought my shunt might be blocked. They decided to "monitor" me and consider "modifying" the shunt.

Jim said I displayed no improvement over the next few days -- no change at all, in fact. The only thing he could note was that I was "following movements with my eyes." Only a month prior to that, I had been walking, dressing myself and brushing my own teeth: rudimentary tasks that had become absurdly monumental to expect from me. I had slipped from their grasp again and no one seemed capable of helping me.

The 100th day was October 14, and it passed quietly. Jim arrived around 9:45 a.m., and I was having a CAT scan. I had a pretty "quiet night -- no seizures." He wrote, "Not much happened today except Meg is still totally unresponsive and there are no answers."

Two weeks later, on October 27, with no definitive plan of action, I was returned to Hilltop.

Around this time, Jim stopped counting the days since I first became ill more than three months before. Using dates instead, he made journal entries only periodically and usually only when a crisis occurred. His entries became more like weekly reports as the weight of it all -- not to mention the impossible task of keeping up with every day demands -- seemed to finally catch up with him. He was just trying to survive, and probably had been for a while. He seemed to be moving forward now without the hope that drove him before. He, in fact, made no notes in November. It must have been a relatively quiet -- if not disheartening -- month. I made very little, or no, progress for him to note. The first in a series of new crises began in December.

"Up to this point, the progress has been slow. Starting from zero strength, but good eye contact and movement, she gradually built strength and responsiveness. Over the weekend (12/3-4) we noticed the breathing, bloodshot eyes and sleepiness. On Monday morning, [December 5] she vomited and ran a super high blood pressure

(210/145). At 4 p.m., they sent her to the hospital for tests and observation. About 5 p.m., she had a seizure. (Naturally, no doctor to be found)! They did a chest x-ray, CAT scan, and blood tests. Her temperature is also elevated (101.5). Tests show nothing...except, of course, elevated white blood count. Urinary infection is back?"

And so began a horrific two weeks of temperatures spiking at 106° and blood pressure elevated to a dangerous high of 210/145. I had another urinary tract infection, pneumonia, and a staph infection of the worst kind (MRSA). Once, my parents said, when they arrived for a visit they found me packed in ice, with the windows thrown open to lower my temperature.

In the midst of all this chaos, our dog, Murphy, became ill, was sick all night, and had to be taken to visit the vet, where she had surgery to remove a stone in her stomach. Things quickly went from "bad" to "worse." Jim rallied his sense of humor, calling the stone our "semi-precious stone," as the cost of the surgery to remove it was quite dear. By contrast, his record of my illness is clinical and almost mechanical, as if he couldn't bear to imagine any of it.

I fought off illnesses and "rode the ventilator" through most of that December. On Christmas

Eve, Jim brought in a boom box with Christmas music and he said it relaxed me enough to allow me to sleep. After the family Christmas party that night, my brother, Mike, took Murphy -- who as a young dog, needed more attention than we could give her -- home to live with him and his family.

Jim spent a quiet Christmas with me. "Brought Meg gift from [our neighbors]...Raven/Murphy stuffed dogs. Cute," he wrote. "Meg has good color, good eye contact and movement. Temp, BP good. Still initiating breathing with ventilator in assist. She seems to be doing more of the work... getting better," he also noted. But the next day, he wrote, "Meg's having problems." He said I had "spiked a temp" and that I looked "very pale and exhausted." My breathing was faster and my blood pressure was low.

Early in my stay at Syracuse, Mike told his friend Eileen how sick I was. She recommended he talk to a neurologist who had helped her after a horse riding accident. Eileen and this doctor lived near each other in Lyme, New Hampshire, and became friends in part because of their mutual love of horses. "Call him. He will help you," Eileen told my brother.

At that point, Jim and my parents felt like they had no one who could help them make important medical decisions. When something happens to someone that you love, you want only the best possible help you can find.

After some encouragement and an initial call to the doctor by Eileen, Mike took a chance and called himself.

Dr. Lawrence Jenkyn was a sympathetic ear and faithful source of information throughout our ordeal. He gave my parents his advice. They so appreciated having a doctor take an interest in my circumstances.

In December, with my health rapidly failing, Jim and my parents contacted Dr. Jenkyn and told him of my dire condition. It was a phone call that quite literally saved my life. Dr. Jenkyn "strongly recommended" that I immediately be brought to Dartmouth-Hitchcock Medical Center in Lebanon, New Hampshire, where he could evaluate me and recommend a course of action.

Had this doctor not agreed to treat me at that time, I would not have recovered to the extent that I have. Certainly, no one else to that point had given me odds of *any* meaningful recovery. This doctor was yet another highly skilled professional in a long list of professionals responsible for my survival and rehabilitation.

I was taken off the ventilator on December 29th, of that year, and despite the persistence of my staph infection, Dartmouth allowed my transfer on January 3.

Up to the day I was moved, Jim never even mentioned it in his journal. He was still in the mechanical "put one foot in front of the other" mode and seemed to have given up anticipating any positive change. Perhaps he was protecting himself from any more crushing disappointments.

I arrived at Dartmouth at 7:10 p.m. and was attended to immediately. For the first time since my transfer to Rutland and subsequent move to Hilltop, Jim began to show his old optimism. He, for the first time in months, had a reason to be excited.

"All is in order," he wrote, "and she's in her room by 7:15 p.m. Mike is here and waiting. At 9:30 p.m., doctors arrived, examined Meg, and had already read her charts! Incredible!" The next day, he added "Met the neurologist at 8:00 a.m. and got initial impression of the team. It sounds encouraging."

Years after the fact, I read this and gave a silent cheer for my husband and the rest of my family. They finally had a little hope to hold onto. There would be more hardships and setbacks to come and a lot of work, but this truly was the turning point for which my husband had prayed.

Chapter 4

Dartmouth

My stay at Dartmouth lasted less than one month, but it laid the foundation for my eventual recovery. Reading about my Dartmouth stay in Jim's journal, it was immediately apparent that there was an increase in my family's confidence in my care. They were still worried about me, but my care there and Dr. Jenkyn's patient, open and honest interaction with them, greatly eased their minds. For the first time in months, their fear and bewilderment was replaced by a strong sense that someone had taken charge of my condition and was charting a course out of the wilderness we all had been wandering in since my AVM had burst.

Even though my health problems continued, Jim's journal entries seemed lighter and more confident. He was even using exclamation points! It was obvious he felt more informed, valued and cared for in this new environment. He had a strong sense that I was in capable hands, as well. On my second day at Dartmouth, he wrote: "Met the neurologist at 8:00 a.m. and got initial impression of team. It sounds encouraging. Could be possible shunt problems to be repaired or a second shunt could be added to relieve pressure on back of the head."

"Lots of tests today. EEG, EKG, MRI, CT, X-Rays. No conclusions at this point. Should have better idea after conferences with doctors. Established 'home' at nearby [motel]."

After my tests were reviewed, it was concluded I needed a shunt revision. Jim wrote what the doctors reported after my surgery: "Did shunt revision this [morning]. All went well. They had to replace entire length. No pressure with old one. When new one was placed, fluid came out under pressure! Sounds like right move. Slept most of day, but eyes look better and more movement with legs and right arm."

I showed good initial improvement according to Jim's records, but three days after my surgery to revise the shunt, he was already being asked to look for new longer-term care for me. "Went to a rehab in Massachusetts with Mike today. Not too impressed," he wrote. "Will look at another one next week."

On January 14, he was at least given a chance to be excited. "Wow. Came in today and Meg is in 'full motion.' Both arms and both legs are moving. She didn't seem agitated, just restless! She looked quite alert, with good eye contact. (This while in bed). Then got up in chair and fell asleep! Haven't been able to catch up to doctors in a while with road trip, etc. Hope to get updated on scans, tests, and observations today."

Over the next few days, my condition didn't change much. Tests showed no seizure activity. Jim wrote: "Neurosurgeon has been monitoring pressure and swelling, and CT scans are questionable at this time. There are no behavioral symptoms to indicate shunt failure, but he's not totally comfortable. Earlier this week, a neurologist tried a couple of drugs to enhance neuro-response. They had very little effect -- so were stopped. Infections are under control and vitals are good."

Although Jim was concerned, he was no longer panicked. He appreciated so much the way the doctors communicated with him and demonstrated their dedication to making me well. They didn't have all the answers, but they were making a great effort and they seemed to show a real interest in me and in my situation.

Even though my immediate problems hadn't yet been resolved, my long-term care was still a big concern. On January 20th, Jim and Mike visited a rehab in Boston. "My feelings were quite ambivalent. These places are all starting to look alike…Promise great things."

Meanwhile, back at Dartmouth, the medical team that was taking care of me kept searching for ways to help me. On January 25th, Jim wrote, "The neurosurgeon reconsidered CT scan and decided to do another shunt revision this [afternoon]. Surgery lasted 1-½ hours and went well. He said when he put in new shunt only a small amount of fluid came out, so he inserted it a little deeper and relieved quite a bit of pressure. He seemed quite optimistic about Meg's prognosis and said areas affected were not critical and he has seen worse cases turn out well. Meanwhile, discharge planner is pressing for transfer. I insist no earlier than Monday."

A few things are notable about these events. First, it would be my last major reparative surgery. Second, the doctors were honest about what they found and encouraging about moving forward. Third, the discharge planner -- prompted by insurance requirements -- was pressuring Jim to move me to a long-term care facility, even as I was coming out of surgery.

How many times was my family hounded during this whole ordeal to move me even as they were struggling with decisions about my immediate health? How often does this happen with families of critically and chronically ill patients? Unfortunately, I truly believe we were the rule and not the exception to it.

Jim persuaded them otherwise and I was not moved for another five days, which was fortunate, since I had problems with nausea and vomiting until then.

I was relocated to the Greenery near Boston on January 30th and spent the next four months there. I remember none of it. Jim remembers it. It was far from home and expensive to stay there. Initially, he was lucky enough to stay with friends, Heidi and Peter, before finding an apartment in Waltham.

With the return of warm weather that spring, Jim would often make the 6-1/2 mile trip to the Greenery in Brighton by bicycle. It made my mother quite nervous, but he found it easier than battling the horrendous traffic around Boston in an automobile.

My parents remember that period of time well. They stayed in the apartment when Jim had to work. Leaving was difficult for him. My condition was still erratic, and he worried about me when he could not be there, but he knew my parents would be watching out for me. They visited me every day.

One morning when they came in, I was agitated over being wet and unchanged. When they complained, the administrators responded by changing the start of visiting hours to later in the day.

I made some progress there but in Mid-March, I started to get lethargic again, so my seizure medicine was decreased. Jim wrote that I "showed improvement rapidly." On March 16, he noted that my "trach was replaced -- didn't downsize," he added. And on the seventeenth, he wrote "Meg's progress is slow and steady. No major medical setbacks. Still has UTI, which is periodically treated with antibiotics. Celebrated Meg's 35th on [March 29]."

Making only one journal entry for the period from April 11th to May 30th, my husband reported that: "Meg was showing some improvement early in this period. Deliberate movement, particularly with hands and arms, was improving. She was also in PT standing class on tilt board...holding head up and moving arms on request. Her seizure medication level has stabilized. Weather is getting good. We're outside as much as possible. As of about May 1, we started to notice a decline in alertness and activity level. This decline is steadily increasing."

On May 19th, I had a CAT scan and the rehab neurologist thought the shunt was working too well and was producing slit-like ventricles or "flattened" ventricles in my brain.

He sent the scan to Dr. Jenkyn, who said not to modify the shunt. Instead, my medication was changed. "Should be less sedating," Jim wrote. Until this point, and for some time in the future, I could not know exactly what my family and friends had been through after my stroke: the new medical terminology they had learned; what they had been exposed to; the people they had met. I was not always cognizant of those things. My recollection of them is "fuzzy" or non-existent.

I was not aware, for example, that I was never alone a single day while I was sick. My husband works four days and is free four days. When he wasn't with me in the hospital or rehab, my parents were. Jim or my parents or both -- along with my brother, various aunts and uncles and cousins were all with me. Employers were all very considerate about the situation and gave them time off when it was needed. This gave them time to visit me in all those hospitals and rehabs.

I also didn't know how very lucky I was with health insurance. Originally, there was a "cap" of $500,000 on my health care. Jim's employer, being self-insured, at the time raised the cap to $750,000. I went through that, and later they raised the limit again to one million dollars. I cannot conceive of my bills totaling that much and I cannot fathom what experiencing this would be like for someone with no or even poor health care benefits.

I was also lucky about all the people who happened into my life and made such a difference in my recovery, even before I had a chance to really meet them. In one very important case, my father met a woman named Mary who was the head of Physical Therapy at Wesley Health Care and Rehabilitation Center, in Saratoga Springs, New York. Working in an office above the local hardware store, whose owner was a friend of Mary's, my father had a chance to speak with her a few times. Learning how far away I was, Mary told my dad about Wesley, which has a floor for young adults and is considerably closer to my home.

Wesley was not easy to get into, but Mary helped set up the initial interviews that were necessary, and on June 2nd, Jim reported that he had, "made arrangements to transfer [me] to Wesley Health Care and Rehabilitation Center in Saratoga Springs, New York." My long journey was finally coming full circle. I would spend the next fifteen months there, and Wesley would provide many more miracles along my path to recovery.

Chapter 5

Wesley

On June 5, I was transferred to Wesley. The transfer, like many aspects of my recovery, was not without its complications: "Was going to use Salem Rescue Squad Ambulance," Jim wrote, "but 4 a.m. that morning, while transferring a patient to Albany Med, they hit a deer. Scrambled to get alternate...Cambridge Rescue loaned [Meg's Uncle] Jack their ambulance. Transfer went well -- no problems. This place is great -- well run and organized. Some problem with trach -- not same brand and no replacement inner cannula."

The next day began on a much higher note and Jim seemed excited to tell about it: "When I got here at 10 am, Meg was up, bathed, and in a fitted chair! WOW -- fast! Some question about trach...brought in Respiration Tech to get it straightened out. Also PT and OT saw Meg a short time. In pm, spoke with speech and social worker for background and medical history. I'm very impressed with care, attitude and efficiency."

Over the next few days, I had some medical complications, including a fever and pneumonia, which Jim wrote only briefly about.

On June 21, when those problems seemed under control, Jim wrote what would be his last journal entry: "Meg had follow-up x-ray yesterday … pneumonia has cleared up. Had trach replaced today. I think it was rougher on the nurses than Meg. She seems quite alert and there's minimal blood in sputum. Therapy is going well. Tracking and using 'yes/no' board really well. Moving legs on command a small amount. Arms not doing much except during cough."

After months of being a patient in places where my family had been concerned about me and about my well-being, they were finally certain of my surroundings and that I would be well tended to there. It had been a long road, and I still had a long way to go. I still had a trach for breathing and a stomach tube for feeding, so I was not ready to live at home yet. I needed the constant care of therapists and nurses and doctors. I also was not yet aware of everything that was going on around me, which in all probability was "nature's way of protecting [me] from traumatic memories" as my neurologist explained to me. Jim and my parents could finally leave at night and be sure to find me in good spirits and good physical condition the following morning.

It must have been a relief, too, that I was close to home, which was only about twenty-five miles away. My parents and Jim were, at last, able to have a more normal life. They could at least sleep in their own beds. No more living out of a suitcase in hotel rooms or rented houses. It also meant getting back to normal work schedules.

Wesley is where I first became aware of what was going on around me, but I didn't simply wake up; it was a very gradual process. At times, I felt like I was drowning. I was at the bottom of a pool of water looking up. I could see blue sky; I knew it was there if I could only get to it, but I could not reach it. When I was unaware, in all probability my brain was healing itself. I was simply "existing" while my brain worked on repairing itself. My brain was simply not observing what was happening around it.

It is a very odd thing and a difficult one to explain, but it was as if I was there and yet I wasn't. Everything felt so strange to me. Just odd. It was very confusing. I really didn't know where

I was, or why I was there. I didn't even realize I was in Saratoga, one of my old stomping grounds.

One thing I do remember from that time was the use of a Hoyer lift to get me out of bed; to put me in my wheelchair, where I could then get dressed, be transferred to the loo, or transported to therapy. The Hoyer Lift, or sling lift, is fashioned after a floor crane used in an automotive shop to lift engines out of automobiles. I knew it was important to protect the workers' backs, but I really disliked that thing. I disliked the way I felt while dangling in the air. It also seemed that it took a long time waiting for the lift and then waiting to be secured in the lift; that I disliked.

People delivered me to therapy sessions and made sure that I was dressed, my face and teeth were clean, and my hair was brushed. Why did I need "therapy" anyway? What had happened? I continually asked my therapists, "When will I get better?" They answered what questions they could and treated me with patience, politeness and understanding.

"PT" was physical therapy, involving gross motor skills. When I attended physical therapy sessions, I exercised on a mat, swam and tried to walk again.

"OT" meant occupational therapy, involving working on fine motor skills. It teaches you how to perform with limitations that you might have acquired -- limitations in performing ADL's or "activities of daily living," in different ways. These include new and different ways to brush your hair or your teeth, or to dress. My brain knows how to do these things, but my body sometimes responds by saying, "No. I'm going to do it like this," and it does something very different. Somewhere between the brain and the muscles, the message gets garbled. The actions and movements that used to be smooth and rhythmical, are now uncoordinated.

There were truly good people that worked at Wesley, some who went "above and beyond the call of duty" to help me out and make me comfortable.

Shortly after I was admitted there, I was introduced to Tammi or "T." She was the physical therapist who was assigned to me by Mary, the department head who was acquainted with my parents. Mary evaluated me and thought Tammi would make a good match. She was correct. My match with Tammi *was* a good one, and my entire family is convinced that Tammi played a major role in my returning health.

I have no memory of those first months at Wesley, however everyone was certain that there was a "spark" between Tammi and me. Something just "meshed."

Mom told me the thing that she remembers the most about Tammi is that Tammi never "gave up" on me. She could always find a little improvement to note on my chart. Months after I was living at home, we were still finding the little yellow pieces of paper that Tammi would leave for Mom, Dad or for Jim, telling them about any progress no matter how miniscule. I had been removed from the therapy schedule for not exhibiting enough response at other rehabs, and it proved to be lucky that Tammi and I were paired from the beginning.

So many other people had given up on me in the past. There was, for example, a doctor that told my mother I could never have my trach removed because it had been there so long. In addition, one occupational therapist discontinued her service to me, because she said I would never "get better."

Tammi, by contrast, seemed incurably optimistic. One of her reports about me written to my family read: "We had a great PT session. For the first time, she fully kicked her right leg up and down without my hands even touching her -- 10Xs. She did all her up and down, side-to-side with her feet without me asking. Also, she raised her right shoulder up with only probably 20% of my help. Excellent day -- very exciting.

Hope all is well,

Tammi"

I find it very hard to believe that someone could be so excited about something so seemingly minor!

A brief synopsis of my relationship with Tammi would be that there really isn't a "brief" synopsis. "T" was there with me even before I was aware of what was going on around me. Being assigned to "T" was another bit of luck in my recovery. It was as if she was my guardian angel... always keeping an eye on me when I couldn't take care of myself.

When I first started "swimming to the surface," I went through a period of not believing anyone around me was real. I didn't know what they were. I couldn't explain it -- maybe they were characters in a story? A dream? They just were not "real." I believe this was probably because at the time I was thinking about myself so much. I probably had to think of myself and my recovery at the time -- I created my "own little world" and I was the only real person in it. All too clearly, I remember wondering how I was going to tell Tammi, my therapist and friend, that she didn't exist. How could I relate that? I could not understand it myself so how could I tell her that she simply didn't exist -- that her thoughts and opinions meant nothing? I really did not want to tell her.

I was with Tammi the first time that Mom heard my voice in a long while. Tammi put money in a pay phone in a hallway at Wesley, held the receiver to my ear and said, "*Talk.*" There was no time to think of not talking. I didn't have much of a voice then; it wasn't exactly melodic (my trach hadn't been gone all that long), but I took the phone, opened my mouth, and said, "*Hi, Mom!*"

Jim said he thought of how Tammi was able to "push my buttons" and really encourage me to work. She would tell me, "You go, girl," and then I would know that I had really accomplished something. In those days, that might have been something as simple as bridging: lifting my butt off the mat while my shoulders and feet stayed down on the exercise mat.

When Jim had a day free from work, he would come to visit me at an earlier hour than my parents could, and he would take me to my occupational therapy session right after breakfast. He would push me in my wheelchair through the halls, past all the other residents' rooms, to the Occupational Therapy room. In the OT room, he would sit quietly until I was finished with whatever task I was working on that day.

One of the tasks that I remember performing there involved a little football that slid on a couple of strings with handles at each end. A therapist held the handles on one end, and I held the handles on the other. The therapist would pull his or her hands far apart, sending the ball hurtling in my direction. If I pulled my hands far apart when the ball was coming toward me, the ball would slow and eventually stop. This exercise taught me eye/hand coordination.

I worked with a few therapists at Wesley. Walter would never accept "uncle" and I did not utter a complaint often. He would continue to push me even when I did complain. I found that most times he was right. I could do *one more* exercise. I wanted to be home. The best incentive for working hard was the silent promise of going home. I just knew that going home was my reward.

In his humorous way, Walter always chided me on my posture, pronouncing it "post-cha" with a British accent, and I found out the hard way it was not without good reason. During one of our sessions, I was exercising on a bench in the PT room when I lifted a foot off the floor and didn't shift my weight correctly; I lost my balance and almost toppled over. Walter dove, catching me milliseconds before I hit the gray linoleum floor.

Jim, Walter and I nervously laughed, and Jim said, "You would do anything to get a football player to fall for you."

That experience will probably always stick with me. How exactly did I go from being a fairly active person -- enjoying biking and skiing, both requiring a great deal of balance -- to someone who almost fell while sitting?

Because Jim's job was in Saratoga, he would sometimes (when he was working at night) come straight to Wesley from work and crawl onto my bed to catch a few winks before I was due in Occupational Therapy. Sometimes Donna, a nurse on our floor who was quite a bit of fun, would put a "Do Not Disturb" sign on the door, and we would let him sleep while I went to breakfast.

Donna was another Wesley person I remember so fondly. She had such an impish personality -- full of fun. It made you wonder, "What *is* she up to?"

Between therapy sessions, I felt really lonely and I just didn't want to be alone. I know it was no one's fault. The staff was spending quite a bit of time keeping me company. Jim and my parents were spending as much time with me as they possibly could: as much as work and life allowed.

One of the brighter events during that time was when Jim's sister, Shirley, came to visit. Since I was able to take short excursions at that point, she decided to take me clothes shopping at a nearby mall. It was such a thrill for me to get away for a while. Once there, my head was on a swivel taking in all the sights and sounds of familiar activity. Shirley later told me that I wanted to buy everything!

On another occasion, Shirley's husband, Larry, came to visit with his young grandsons, Addam and Andrew. I remember this visit because the boys started getting restless and bored. The nurses took them out of the room and entertained them by running up and down the halls while Larry and I talked.

One of the aides, Bridget, had a great smile and was so nice. When she was working, she was always so cheerful and made the time pass more quickly. She even named her baby after me! Her name was Gabrielle Megon! Everyone commented on the fact that she was called Gabby Megon, and that was exactly what I became once I finally began talking again. (I believe my family thought I became a bit too "gabby.")

Cindy was the nurse in charge of my floor when Wesley was my home. I used to go to her office, sit quietly while she did paperwork and wait for my parents to arrive after they left their work for the day. I needed a lot of company at the time. I liked to have someone near me at all times during my recovery.

Another person who looked after me was Flo, who was an aid on our floor. After my parents or Jim left for the night, she would sit with me and keep me company until I fell asleep. It was a sad time of day -- a quiet and lonely time. I was also restless and didn't sleep well.

Mary, a nurse on my floor, was interested in computers. It gave Jim, who shared Mary's interest, something to do when he visited. He could at least "compare notes" with her, and I think it made the days pass a little faster for him. Computers were pretty foreign to me.

We had purchased a computer for the greenhouse business the year that I "got sick", so I never had the chance to learn the things that Jim and Mary talked about. The computer actually arrived just after I was hospitalized. It was confusing to hear Jim and Mary talk, because I couldn't understand how Jim knew all of those things and I didn't. I was not yet cognizant of my lost time.

Before my trach was removed, I became very aware of exactly how essential it is to communicate. We communicate our wants and needs, mostly with our voice. When that means is gone, quite a bit has been taken from us. We want to express ourselves, but are just not able to do it.

My family and I went through several different methods of communication while I lived at Wesley, finally deciding on a letter board early on. I "graduated" to its use from the "Yes/No" board in which I could only be asked questions answered by a "Yes" or "No." Then, I would glance towards the correct answer. The board was difficult and arduous to use, but it *was* a way to be understood. I remember that I carried that board around with me at all times. It provided a means to "talk" with other people! *I could communicate!*

The letter board was divided into four quadrants. I would look towards a quadrant and whomever I was "conversing" with would guess what letter it was that I wanted, and I would spell out the words. I remember wondering how whomever I was "talking" with could ever be correct. It seemed that their guess was usually "right on the mark," although, it *was* a laborious task. Mom told me that they weren't really correct all that often.

I had absolutely no idea how long I used that communication board. It could have been weeks or it could have been days. I had no concept of time then. My "coming back" was so gradual -- a *gradual awareness*. There was nothing clear and defined in my mind. Jim told me later that I had used the board for a couple of months.

After the letter board, we all learned to sign with our hands. One of Jim's co-workers brought us a plastic place mat that showed us the symbols. It pictured all the signs and how we should hold our hands. We would refer to the place mat when we wanted to sign. It was not easy. It did give us some good results, though.

To make it all a little easier, we used a couple of shortcuts. The sign for the letter "t" meant that I needed the bathroom, or toilet, and my arms crossed across my chest meant, "I love you": two very important things at that point in my recovery. They pretty much said everything I needed to say.

Most of my intentions and desires were nearly impossible to convey. Sometimes it was frustrating -- there was so much we all wanted to tell each other. It became a guessing game for my visitor -- like playing charades!

During that time, Jim gave me a little figurine that I treasured. It was an angel figurine demonstrating the sign of love that we all had learned to use -- arms crossed across the chest.

Eventually doctors, nurses, and therapists began to notice that I was breathing around my trach. Air was going around it as well as through it.

This led my speech therapist to introduce the Passy-Muir Speaking Valve. The Passy-Muir Valve is a one-way check valve that allows you to bring air in through the trach but plugs the trach when you exhale, forcing air up the throat and through the voice box.

It was developed, with the help of Dr. Victor Passy, by David Muir, a quadriplegic with a trach who was a muscular dystrophy patient. The Passy-Muir Valve makes it possible for ventilator patients to speak again.

With it, I began making sounds. Soon, with the help of my Speech Therapist, Janet, I was beginning to form words for the first time in close to two years. I could finally communicate verbally -- at least a bit. Jim said it was great to hear my voice and to finally understand my wishes without guessing.

When I first started talking, Jim would push me in my wheelchair through the Wesley parking lot. To practice speaking, I would recite license plates and count cars in Swedish. I wasn't speaking conversationally yet, but I was at least reciting something and using my vocal cords. I was making sounds. Then they couldn't convince me to remain quiet! It just seemed so good to be talking again! I became a bit too talkative.

One day, Theresa, who was a young aide and a lot of fun, told a joke that I repeated for my parents and my Aunt Barbara and Uncle Jack when they arrived that afternoon. I started telling the joke in the parking lot at their car, continued through the lobby of my building, and up in the elevator, down the hall, and finished in my room. By the end of the joke, we were all laughing. I think they were laughing at my laughing, and I was laughing at the fact that it was the first time in a long time that I had been able to repeat anything of any length and to actually form words.

I was "out of practice," and it felt really good to be talking again! It was the first time I had been able to say *anything* of any length since I "got sick." It seemed odd that I would have to relearn something as basic as how to talk. Those muscles had not been used, and I had to learn to "stretch" them again.

It took at least fifteen minutes for me to tell that joke, which was a bit questionable! It was soon after I began talking, so I'm really not sure how much anyone could understand. Theresa, however, was surprised and embarrassed that I had recovered enough to repeat it. At that point, I hadn't yet talked to anyone other than our family. Theresa could not believe that I told my parents that joke and kept saying that she was "really gonna be in trouble" and would "lose her job." My parents assured her that they thought it was funny, so ultimately she had a good laugh, too.

My speech therapist did more than get me talking. She also worked with cognitive areas, such as telling time and simple math equations, where I was having difficulty. Performing simple tasks like adding a column of figures, subtracting, multiplying or dividing made no sense to me. I truly could not do them.

For example, I couldn't figure out how to "carry" a number, or where to put the number that should be carried, or even remember the number that I wanted to move. I honestly could not keep it in my mind. Janet worked patiently with me while I tried to rebuild the skills and hold onto and retrieve my thoughts.

It was during one of my sessions with her that Janet and I discovered that I had "lost" all of that time when I was "sick." When I think about that day, I *still* hear the conversation.

At one point, Janet asked me, "How much does a stamp cost?" I told her, and she said, "Interesting. What year is it?" I told her the year I thought it was: the year of my AVM. "Interesting," she said. I must have looked very confused. "Meg," Janet said to me, "it's two years later than that."

What an awakening! I had absolutely *no* idea that time had passed! Before that, I thought I could and *would* pick up my life where I had left it. There was no reason to think I couldn't. I will always remember the feelings I had at that moment! It was a turning point for me. Things finally began to make sense. I had lost time.

Almost two years were just gone. Missing. I didn't know what happened to them, but I suddenly remembered an expression from years before. "The penny dropped."

I was a Rotary Exchange Student in Sweden for a year following my high school graduation. The expression "the penny dropped" came to mind at that time because Jan, my Swedish teacher in Stockholm, used to say it quite regularly when someone or everyone in the class finally grasped something.

It's like saying, "The light bulb came on," or "now I understand." That day in therapy, the penny had indeed dropped. I can still hear Jan using that expression in Stockholm, and I wonder if he has any idea of the impact he has had on my life. My Swedish teacher's little bit of insight continues to help me define and understand my discoveries a little better now as I learn more about what happened to me along my path to recovery.

Chapter 6
Ready to Go Home

With my improving verbal skills, I was able to more quickly and easily develop friendships with other people living at Wesley. Glen, who was my cheerleader there, was so important to me -- to all of us. He had been in a car accident when he was much younger, and was still using a wheelchair. He wasn't able to form words, so a computer verbalized for him. He entered the words he chose to say and the computer would turn his words into audible speech.

Glen was extremely happy for me when I finally started talking. With his computer gone, he pounded excitedly on his tray because that was the way he could best express himself. Making noise! Glen was even happier when I taught him to swear in Swedish! Jim and I would hear him coming down the hall with his machine swearing away. It was a good outlet for some of his frustrations, and no one knew what he was saying!

One night, when my parents were still there, Glen and Linda, another resident from our floor, stopped by and we broke into an off-key rendition of "How Much is that Doggy in the Window?" Linda and I sang and Glen played, "Arf! Arf!" In the appropriate place on his computer. We had so many laughs, which was good medicine for all of us!

The staff at Wesley tried to provide other entertainment. There were tropical fish in aquariums near the therapy rooms and near the nurses' stations on each floor. I think they were supposed to provide stimulation. They were fun to watch, anyway.

My parents brought Dunbar (my big black lab) to visit once. Only once. That was the kind of stimulation I needed! Something familiar! But, he nonchalantly backed into the bushes at the edge of the courtyard and relieved himself with half of Wesley looking on!

Less amusing was the parakeet, named HoJo, who lived in a cage on our floor. He was there as a community pet and was supposed to provide additional stimulus to all the residents. I disliked him and all the noise that he made. I thought it was just me that was alone in my dislike for him until one day when I wheeled out to the main nurse's station. There was his cage with a towel thrown over it, so he would think it was night and go to sleep. I guess someone else thought he was a bit noisy, too.

Until then, I thought my hearing, which had become much more acute while I was still living at Wesley, caused my dislike. Probably my hearing was compensation for my poor eyesight. My vision was so bad. I had trouble reading -- even with glasses and a hand lens -- which would have made time pass faster.

I love to read cookbooks and have quite a collection at home. I would read them from cover to cover as if they were novels. However, after the AVM, words appeared to be really tiny and I could not read them. I would stare at the words not quite making them out. I realized I was guessing at the words, when sometimes they didn't seem to "go" where I tried to use them. I would try and try, but I could not quite make them out.

When I first began seeing a neuro-optometrist, my eyesight was corrected to 20/100. Large print books and magazines helped, but I also had trouble keeping my eyes in one plane. They tended to bob around, making it impossible to follow a line. The doctor gave me exercises to do to strengthen my ocular muscles and increase the mobility in my eyes. I was told to hold a piece of paper or other straight edge under the line I was trying to read. It helped, but I was also experiencing double vision. I usually closed one eye to compensate. If I reached out to pick up a pill, for example, I saw two pills and was unsure of which pill to pick up! If I closed one eye, I saw one pill again. (When we saw the July 4th fireworks in my hometown that year, I decided, in that case, seeing double wasn't such a horrible thing!)

Other symptoms plagued me. Sweet things tasted salty to me. There is nothing good about that in my opinion! I attributed this to the AVM and how messages are being rerouted in the brain. Mom reminded me that it may also have been the medication I was taking. I think I blame too much on the AVM. Almost everything, in fact.

I also didn't feel heat with my right hand, which could have been rather problematic. I discovered this once when I was washing my hands and I realized that I couldn't tell the temperature of the water with the right hand. I would feel for the temperature with my left hand first and then put both hands under the water.

One of my many difficulties and a hurdle I had to clear before going home was my dependence on a feeding tube, which delivered "food" from a machine directly to my stomach. I remember once at Wesley when the machine ran out of liquid and it started making the high-pitched humming and beeping noise that I had learned to hate so much. It sounded like a hand-held computer game to me, and to this day, I cannot stand the incessant beeping from video games.

I decided to go somewhere that would disguise the noise from that machine. The lunchroom! I would leave my quiet room and find some company. That would do it! There would be enough chatter in the dining room that it would probably mute that terrible droning machine. The activity there would at least keep me from hearing every last beep.

I was once wheeling my way to the lunchroom, pulling the machine along with me, when it fell over! I tried, but I couldn't stand it up again. It was too heavy for me and it was also in an awkward position, so I couldn't hoist it upright. I have never felt such frustration!

At that very time, I heard a familiar voice: Dave from the maintenance department. He was one of those good people at Wesley who always seemed to show up when I was in need of help. Always cheerful, always helpful, he came and picked the machine up from the terrazzo floor where it lay. He began to tell me how expensive the machine was. He stopped, however, when he saw how distressed I was already. People like Dave made Wesley easier to bear, but incidents like that made me more determined than ever to rid myself of that machine. The only way to do that was to pass a swallow test.

I had already failed the swallow test once since coming to Saratoga. The test consisted of swallowing different textures and thicknesses of various foods. I simply didn't have the muscles I needed to control my swallowing, and I aspirated food. Residues came out of the trach tube and onto my neck. I don't remember taking that first test at all. I simply wasn't aware then. It was given at a hospital that was only about 10 miles away from where I was living.

At that time, my young nephew, Sean, would not accept a hug from me because he said, "I spit on him!" (Residues came out my trach and were deposited on my chin or on anything I came into contact with.) How confusing this was for him!

It is hard to understand how doctors believe you could possibly pass the swallow test without practice when you have not eaten food in a long time. I hadn't used those muscles in almost two years!

After that, my family helped me practice in my room. My bathroom door and the door to the corridor opened into each other, blocking the view from the hallway. We would position the doors this way while my family fed me a teaspoon or two of pudding, so I could exercise my swallowing muscles with some privacy. With the door partially open, someone from the staff would be able to hear if I had a problem and coughed, and they stayed within earshot to assist if necessary. How grateful we are to them for their help!

I did pass the test the second time, and then *did* have the trach surgically removed.

I remember looking up at the doctor who was about to remove my trach, and I really wanted to comment on his silly hat, which looked like a paper shower cap. Then I touched my own head and realized that I was wearing one, too! It took me a minute, but I then realized that it is the hat you wear to contain your hair during an operation.

What a day it was when the feeding tube finally came out! I wouldn't need to have my food in a special solution any longer. I could eat regular food all the time and I could eat through my mouth! I didn't realize it then, but it was another step in my going home.

When I began eating again, all of my food had to be pureed in a blender or food processor. The sight of it seemed to bother others more than it bothered me. I didn't find it offensive at all. Almost everything tasted good; appearances simply didn't matter. Probably because it had been so long since I had eaten food. I still had no true concept of time, so I didn't know if I had eaten a day or a year before then. Apparently my taste buds knew though.

It really is astonishing what you can put in a blender and puree! Pizza was even good -- the flavor was there. You just had to get past the sight of it, which really was not particularly appetizing. I learned to close my eyes and imagine how it would appear in a big, round pan! Pesto sounded good, and I talked about that until Jim brought me some. I even had a lobster tail in butter a la blender as one of my first meals on a weekend visit home!

I could also have chopped ice to "drink." We had to add a thickener to everything I did drank. Without it, liquids would go down too easily and make me cough and perhaps choke. The thickener had no flavor, but it didn't look great -- not at all appetizing. It had a rather strange consistency. Everything I drank had the consistency of a smoothie. The thickener appeared gray in water but couldn't be detected in most liquids.

After pureed food came chopped. It was regular food that had been cut up into very small pieces. It was the next step in my going home for good. I began eating "chopped" at Wesley and continued after I arrived home. Jim informed me that it was several months of eating chopped food at Wesley and then at home. I was not aware of that at all. I still had no clear concept of time. Time seemed to vanish at that point in my recovery, so I thought that I stayed there eating "chopped" for a short period of time -- days or weeks perhaps, certainly not the months Jim said it was.

One of the first chopped foods I remembered eating during my recovery were green beans in the lunchroom at Wesley. (I couldn't even feed myself then. I could not "find" my mouth with the utensil. I thought, however, that it was my father feeding me. Much later, Mom told me that *she* had fed me, so I guess my memories of that time are not yet clear.)

I do remember going to the lunchroom each day and assessing that day's dinner selection. I thought most of the food there was good -- quite palatable. However, if that evening's selection didn't appeal to me, I had a back-up plan. When my parents arrived for the evening, I would tell them, "It looks like an ice cream kinda night." Dad would go and get ice cream for us at a local soft serve place. I remember this vividly because I always asked for their pistachio ice cream. Pistachio is not a flavor I would normally enjoy or ever choose, but this particular soft serve appealed to me in some way.

As I became better able to eat and my health improved, "overnighters" from Wesley became weekend visits home. I remember that Sunday nights were not easy on any of us. The rides back to Wesley were long, sullen ones. Wesley was a good facility, but it was very difficult to leave home behind. It was so comforting to have my own things -- a familiar feeling and place. My family and dogs were there and I was determined to be there too.

I celebrated that Mother's Day while still living in the health care facility in Saratoga. Jim asked me if I wanted to find something for my mom. We went to the gift shop with me riding in my chair and Jim walking along behind, but off to the side a bit where I could see him. (One of my therapists suggested we "walk" like that so I could be more aware of his presence.)

The gift shop was on the first floor of our building. We went down in the elevator. Jim asked me to push the floor button for the mental and physical activity involved.

We arrived at the gift shop and I chose several small gifts for my mother. One of which was a guardian angel pin. I can still picture it, because my niece and nephew gave my mother the very same pin that Mother's Day. I remember that it really bothered me at the time. That piece of jewelry was special and unique, I thought. It did not occur to me that some other store could sell the very same type of pin! My life revolved around Wesley then, and I seemed not to know that the outside world would have the same merchandise. To me, that world didn't exist.

Before I was discharged that September, most of the department heads at Wesley inspected my home and my parents' home -- evaluating the two places where I would be living. They wanted to be certain that the two houses would be prepared for my arrival, that I could navigate them safely, and that I could be as independent as possible in them. I will always remember those "home evals," as they were called, because they determined whether or not I could go home.

After the home evals, Wesley concluded that I no longer required constant medical care and I was able to live at home. Jim's strange "four days on, four days off" work schedule finally seemed right for us. When Jim was working for twelve hours, I could stay with my parents, who resided nearby. When he was free from work, I could live in Cambridge with him. Mom retired so she could spend more time with me when Jim was working.

Before I was discharged from Wesley, I had an appointment at Dartmouth with my neurologist, Dr. Jenkyn. He wanted to examine me and discuss my future treatment and therapy. I had several things to discuss with him, too. I carried a list I had compiled.

From the moment I "became aware," I had been trying to understand what, exactly, had happened to me, and why I was residing at Wesley. Until that point in time, I didn't know exactly what had happened to me. I arrived at Dr. Jenkyn's office armed with my list of questions.

Dr. Jenkyn took my list and read each question out loud.

At some point, I suppose I heard someone near me use the word "stroke," so I wrote that question on my list. "Did I have a stroke?" Dr. Jenkyn quoted from my list. He put the paper down, looked at me and then said, "Yes."

I remember silently crying for a couple of seconds. "I'm sorry," I said to my family. "I didn't know."

Up to that point, I had no idea that what everyone had called an "AVM" or a "bleed," was in reality a "stroke." That word, "stroke," just sounded bad; worse to me somehow than an AVM, which was also known as a cerebrovascular accident. That phrasing seemed strange. To me, there was nothing "accidental" about it. It felt much more like an attack -- unprovoked and unexpected.

I thought strokes were something only the elderly have. I was young. I certainly didn't qualify. When it happened, I was only thirty-four and in very good physical condition. I worked out almost every day and my business kept me active as well. There was also no family history.

Strokes affect people differently, depending on where the injury occurs in the brain. I recall an elderly woman who lived in my hometown when I was growing up. She had had a stroke at some point, and her mouth was badly twisted. I found it very strange that there was no outward sign that I had had a stroke, other than the wheelchair that I used. I remember that I kept asking if I looked different. I couldn't see myself clearly in a mirror because my vision was -- and still is -- impaired, but I was certain my appearance was different.

On the morning that I was due to leave Wesley, Dan, who was an aide on our floor, came into my room as I was waiting for someone to come and get me out of bed. He began to sing the Bette Midler song, "Wind Beneath My Wings." The words said something about me being a "hero." When he got to that part, I was sobbing. I didn't feel much like a hero. I just wanted to go home.

I remember thinking about the words to that song and thinking about all the heroes that I would miss. The people that had taken care of me were my heroes, as well as some of the residents on our floor. Thank heaven there is a place like Wesley, with its caring staff, to live. Not all rehabs are like Wesley.

My friends at Wesley gave me a big going away party with great food and a karaoke machine. We all sang "It's My Party," with the line, "and I'll cry if I want to." We sang that song more than once that afternoon, and we did cry.

I looked around the room at the familiar faces there, realizing I had spent quite a bit of time with many of them even if I didn't remember all of it. There was Donna, who reminded me of how many times Dad and Glen would sneak away and watch a Boston Red Sox game on television. There was Theresa, who told the joke that I repeated, which made everyone believe that maybe it was time for me to live at home. There was Cindy, with whom I had spent so many afternoons waiting for my parents to arrive and who was so instrumental in my getting a maple tree that "could grow with me" and mark my arrival home.

Tammi, who had spent so much time helping me, was there. She called me her "little bird" then, because I was the first resident to go home -- the first to leave the nest. I saw Connie, who had so often sat at our table in the dining room to be sure we all cleaned our plates. Glen was also there to cheer me on. I was, of course, sorry to be leaving him and my other friends behind. I told everyone that I would miss the people -- not the place. I really wanted to be home.

I was the first "inmate" (as I called us) from my floor to go home. I called us inmates, because some residents who were not supposed to go outside alone, had something attached to their wheelchairs that would trigger an alarm and close the doors if they approached them too closely. Whenever I heard that alarm, I would chant, "Go, go, go," to cheer the "escapee" on.

I still feel that some of the nurses were a little glad to see the back of my head as I waved good-bye. They assured me that they were only happy for me, but I think not. I believe they also might have been a bit relieved that their resident militant would not be around to stir things up anymore.

I remember thinking that Jim and my parents must have really wanted me home. It was quite a responsibility just getting me there. I was not easy to take care of. I still needed to have quite a bit done for me. I could not completely feed myself yet, and was not completely dressing myself yet. It seemed that there were others on our floor that were "better" than I was, and they were certainly more mobile, so why weren't they living at home? Luck and the love of my family, was certainly with me.

I understand that, since that time, others have been able to go home. What a great hurdle to clear. The care at Wesley was outstanding, but there is nothing like being home with your own family and your own things.

I will always be grateful to my husband and parents, along with my other relatives, for the love and support that they have given me. My doctors and nurses think this has been crucial for my recovery. The most important thing I needed was their encouragement. It is also so valuable to have an advocate -- someone that can make decisions for me. I was not capable of making decisions for a long time. There were times when my "Irish temper" would flare, but my family stuck by me. They were, truly, my biggest heroes.

Chapter 7
Back Home

My family and friends gave me a "welcome home" party at our house in Cambridge. We had a big tent and everyone from our hamlet, as well as several of Jim's co-workers and our friends and relatives, stopped by for some food and conversation. A friend's dad stood watch over the grill and made sure everyone had a burger. It was wonderful to see so many people who had shown such concern during my illness. It is so important to know that people do care and to have them around you.

My party was held during the day and continued into the evening. It was fortunate that we had that tent, because as the night wore on, the rain moved in and fell in proverbial buckets.

I cannot remember a great deal from that party but, as a chocoholic, I *do* remember the 5-pound chocolate bar that one of Jim's co-workers brought to the party. The memory of it is so strong I can almost taste it.

I wish I could remember other things like I remember that chocolate bar. With whom did I talk? Who was there? What food did I eat? What did I see and look closely at? Did I look around at the people that were there at the party? Did I study the greenhouses that I hoped to work in? Did I glance at the house that I longed to get back to -- that held my books and personal items, not to mention our dog, and of course, Jim? I remembered very little, except for that chocolate bar!

I do remember being worried that Jim wouldn't or couldn't, think of me in the same way -- that he would always think of me as the child I had become. The child who needed to be taken care of and that needed so much attention. It was up to me to make Jim see me as the adult I once was. I could only do that by doing as much as possible for myself. I had hoped, at that time, that I could strike the phrases "I need" and "I want" from my vocabulary, even if I knew that I could not. There was still so much I couldn't do for myself, and maybe never would be able to do again.

Unfortunately, being "discharged" did not mean what I had silently hoped -- that I would be "well" again or "fixed." It simply meant that I no longer needed a nurse's or a doctor's constant care.

When I first arrived home, I couldn't do much for myself. I wasn't even completely feeding myself. I still had a long way to go with many more hours of therapy and exercise ahead of me. I needed quite a bit of care, and I depended on Mom and Dad and on Jim for that: care and encouragement.

Even though I appreciate them, having Mom and Dad and Jim as my primary caregivers made me angry that I even *needed* a caregiver at all, and I sometimes lost my temper. I wondered why I hadn't improved more. I have always had to work hard to achieve most things, but I was used to seeing results when I *did* work hard: the results that I wanted to see and strived for. I expected things to "go my way." I felt anger and confusion and frustration because things did not work as they were supposed to work. Even now I tell myself, "Tomorrow I'll be better." "Tomorrow" just hasn't come yet.

Early on, I did not know what my hands and arms would do, which was a difficult thing for a perfectionist to accept. Sometimes they wouldn't go where I aimed them, which was why eating and other tasks were so baffling. Worse, occasionally they seemed to act of their own accord.

My father "wore" my coffee once, because he didn't tighten the cup lid enough to be certain it was secure. The scene was sheer chaos. My hand shot in his direction. He reached out to intercept the cup, so I wouldn't burn myself with the hot liquid, and instead centrifugal force carried the hot liquid out of the cup and onto his hand and arm.

I also found that I absolutely could not be hurried. I used to thrive on pressure in the past: attending Cornell and then running a business. Now, I'm almost always late for wherever I need to go. The more I hurry to dress and get ready for something, the longer it seems to take. I seem to fumble things like an unlucky football player fumbles a ball.

Other things that should be simple have become difficult. My spelling had always been so good, it seemed so easy, and after the AVM I had a really hard time remembering how to spell some words. I have forgotten things that seemed automatic before. I couldn't remember if it was "I before E" or "E before I." I also couldn't remember the thing about months... "Thirty days has September..." To make matters worse and more confusing, I had a difficult time with current events in my own life. My short-term memory was not good. I would ask the day and date continuously and did not realize that I had just asked the same questions thirty minutes before. Sometimes it was seconds before. How patient everyone was to tell me the day and date so many times.

My long-term memory, however, remained intact. I remembered my high school locker number and combination, my Cornell I.D. number, various phone numbers, including my Swedish phone number…but only in Swedish! I also remembered the Swedish language. That old story of "not remembering what you had for dinner" was definitely true for me. I didn't remember much about dinner, but I did remember my Swedish from twenty years before then!

It was fortunate that I didn't lose my long-term memory. It was important to me to retain some memories of my old life. The doctors told my parents that people who have strokes do sometimes have the problem of losing their long-term memory. Some lucky people have no memory loss.

What I had was considered a brain injury, or a "cerebrovascular accident," which didn't make a lot of sense to me. I didn't feel "injured" was the proper definition of my problem. I simply couldn't remember some things, and my body didn't want to do what it was told -- in-coordination. I didn't feel pain or discomfort. I didn't even have a headache and seldom ever did. I, therefore, didn't feel injured.

The AVM also didn't seem to be too accidental. I felt like it chose me. It somehow decided exactly when the bleed would occur and where.

There are words, such as "outpatient" versus "inpatient," that have become a part of my every day vocabulary. I was an "inpatient" when I lived in the rehabs and an "outpatient" after I went home and returned for therapy appointments. (Before my illness, I was never known for being "patient" at all!)

My family and I regularly used other, more technical medical terminology as well. Somehow, I knew the meanings of all those new words. I knew where and how they should be used in a sentence. I seemed to understand them.

There was the term "AVM" itself. To my knowledge, I had never even heard of an AVM. Now, it played a major role in my life. Everything revolved around the fact that I had had one. Things either happened before the AVM or after.

It had become a "benchmark," as my graduation from high school or college, or my marriage, used to be. It is an integral part of my life now.

I knew what a "bleed" was and I accepted the fact that I had had one. How strange that I talked about it like I knew what it was!

Also, I knew how to use my wheelchair without any apparent instruction. I don't remember when that happened. Did someone have to teach me that, or did it come naturally… because I had seen it before? Of course, my skill in moving my chair can be seen in the woodwork in our house… it sometimes has a "chewed up" appearance.

Then there was the word "ataxia," which is a lack of muscular control and loss of coordination. I had quite a bit of ataxia when I tried to do most things, including something as simple as brushing my hair. I didn't "shake" all the time, but when I tried to do something, I often did not have the coordination necessary to do it.

My ataxia was more "loss of control" than "shaking," as one of my therapists described it. It was uncontrolled movement. I might put my hand out to touch something and the hand would actually come down in a place other than where I wanted it to come down. I felt as if I had no control over my extremities, especially when they were not close to my body. I would brace my arms against my body for additional support. That didn't work, though, if I wanted to reach for something. Then my arms would swing almost uncontrollably back and forth, side to side. I would, sometimes, hold one arm with the other hand so it would waver less.

It seemed that the more I concentrated and the more I tried to do something, the more ataxia I had. That made writing very difficult, if not impossible. I usually couldn't read my own writing, so I couldn't hope anyone else could read it either. It was another means of communication that had slipped away, becoming difficult or impossible for me.

There also seemed to be "good days" when I had a bit more control and I felt better than the "bad days" when everything was difficult. On the bad days, I learned it was better to "just accept it" -- another difficult thing for me to do.

Mom often says "light touch" to me now. When I am eating, I still tend to grasp things too tightly. It is as if I cannot regulate how hard I grasp things. "Light touch" is supposed to remind me to take it easy and not squeeze. It is not that I really need reminding. I know what I want to do, but actually doing it is something very different. "Light touch" does, usually, make me move slower, which helps.

Sandwiches have been quite challenging; I squeeze them and the insides "squirt out. " Forget eating an ice cream cone. They are impossible for me to eat. The cones shatter in my vice-like grip, as do potato chips, so I just don't eat them!

Whenever I eat out, I study the menu, or I have someone else read it for me (I am not very fast and still have a problem with my eyesight). I attempt to decide what would be easiest to eat -- something I can eat with a fork or a spoon.

When I first became aware and even more so when I moved home, I felt out of place -- like I didn't quite belong. Several things made big impressions on me as I tried to fit back in. They may seem trivial -- my impressions -- but they are things I have thought about quite a bit. Things really have changed a great deal.

For instance, many people own cell phones now. They run around like Maxwell Smart from "Get Smart." I sometimes call these phones "beam me up phones," because they remind me of "Star Trek" and "Beam me up, Scottie!" I found it really strange that voices are floating around out there, and huge towers pick them up.

There are so many different phone companies now, as well. In my memory, there were only two or three you heard about. It's a bit overwhelming now!

Seeing people everywhere, running around with bottles of water that they paid money for was really odd to me as well. Strangers walking by, phone in one hand, bottled water in the other, were like people from a future I had suddenly been dumped into.

The routine use of PCs was new to me, too. Since the computer we had ordered for the greenhouse business didn't arrive until after my AVM, I never saw it until my first home visit.

The word "website" didn't mean anything to me (unless, of course, it had something to do with a spider!). A "site" was, for example, The Statue of Liberty...something to be seen. "Surfing the net" was new to me too. "WWW" has made so much information available that it has become a topic of everyday conversation. I had never heard of that before. Wherever I went, it seemed people were talking about information they discovered "on the Net."

I did a lot of smiling and nodding when I first "woke up," because I had never heard of many things.

Doctors and hospitals didn't advertise. It just wasn't done. I remember wondering how that became accepted. I still think that is an odd thing.

Forget about grocery shopping. I always had to ask whomever I was with if "it's a good price." The price of beef, for example, has really increased. It is good that I'm partial to chicken!

The prices aren't the only thing that changed. Strangely, some seemingly inconsequential things, like the outward appearance of dish soap bottles, really bothered me. Now, there are short, squat bottles; they all used to be tall and narrow. Also, the packages of toilet paper have increased by size and quantity. There also seems to be a lot of dollar stores with many different names.

Speaking of names, somehow the Houston Oilers became the Tennessee Titans. It wasn't that I was such a big football fan. I wasn't. The name was just different and that bothered me.

I don't remember the Oklahoma City bombing or the O.J. Simpson trial (but I do remember the chase of his vehicle when he was arrested).

Jim bought me a cookbook and the proceeds were to benefit the foundation of a local girl that had disappeared. Her disappearance was during the time that I was having memory problems so how, then, did I remember her? I remembered some things, but not other things. This added to the confusion.

It is possible that I knew about her disappearance subconsciously, because of all the media coverage at the time. The television was always left on in my room to provide a little background noise. Maybe my brain absorbed the information somehow.

Before my illness, songs on the radio were always quite important to me. I would listen and sing along. They were great company when I was working alone in the greenhouse or driving alone to deliver plants to customers.

When I first "woke up" at Wesley, I wasn't familiar with the popular songs. I wasn't even familiar with some of the artists. That should have been an indication of what had taken place, but it still was not.

When I left Wesley to live at home, we gave a CD player to the residents on my floor and one CD to start their collection. Dan, the aid on our floor who sang for me when I left Wesley said, "I've heard good things about this one," in reference to the CD. To me, it seemed like it was an odd thing to say, because that was a very popular CD, wasn't it? As it turned out, it was popular when I got sick. I was still thinking in the past. The CD was "Eric Clapton: Unplugged." I think I will always associate it with going home.

You hear the phrase "seeking closure" now. You didn't hear that phrase much before. Now, it's used quite often, as is "went missing." I tried to remember what we said before. I guess it was "disappeared."

Then, there are word uses that didn't appear as often earlier. I don't find it possible to incorporate "awesome" or "issue" into my every day vocabulary. They appear so frequently now, but we didn't use them before, so I don't use them much now. At first, it even bothered me to hear them -- another thing that was different.

These things may not seem like much to anyone else -- certainly not important, but they are just a few of the things that I have noticed. I called it "The Rip Van Winkle Syndrome." When I "fell asleep" things were one way, and when I "woke up" they were another way.

I tend to think of the time I was unresponsive as the time I was "asleep" because I wasn't communicating. I wasn't cognizant of anything that was happening around me, and I also was not cognizant of anyone.

I probably find it more bothersome that things are not the way they used to be. Some things do not even sound the same. There are times that I draw a complete blank. What a strange feeling... to have a blank space in my memory. I hear "I told you that" and I don't have a memory of the topic at all.

One day, I noticed a scar on my wrist that I had no memory of, so I asked Jim about it. He could only tell me that it was from "a machine" that I was "hooked up to" when I was in the hospital in Syracuse. I wanted to know who had attached the machine and what its purpose was. I touched the scar briefly and it troubled me, I think, because it was a reminder of all the people whom I have met along the way that I have no memory of meeting. I need to know exactly what occurred. I am simply so curious about it.

There were so many blank spaces in my mind regarding my care during those months when I was unaware of my surroundings. It seemed that my recovery could not be complete until I had all the answers to my questions. There were, and are, so many of them.

Our dog, Raven (one of our black labs) was a great comfort to me when I first arrived home -- a familiarity. She seemed to know how confused I was and realized that I needed daily assurances. I could talk to her and she listened as if she understood.

At one time, we had three black labs: Raven, Dunbar and Murphy. Due to the infamous rock-swallowing incident, Murphy went to live with my brother's family. Dunbar, who was our first dog when Jim and I got married, passed away soon after I returned home. Maybe he was waiting for me to return first, since he was quite old.

At first, Dunbar didn't take much notice of me. He almost seemed to have forgotten me. The day that he died, though, he came over, leaned against my chair and wanted me to pet him.

We were at my parents' house that evening and after I talked to him for a while, he went outside, walked the perimeter of the yard, and then simply lay down under a plum tree. My parents could see what was happening but didn't want to alarm me. When they finally realized that he had stopped breathing, they told me. I guess it was good that I couldn't see what was taking place, and had no idea what was happening with him.

Dunbar's passing was a painful reminder of the things that I had missed. Two years is a long time in the life of a dog. Two years is a long time in the life of a person. Time that I could never get back.

Chapter 8

Our Labs

For the two of us, the one constant in our married life has been our Labrador Retrievers. I have already mentioned three of them. At one time, we had two adult dogs and eight puppies. Dunbar, who came to live with me before we were married, was with us until shortly after I returned from Wesley. He was a sweet dog who didn't know quite what to do when I arrived home, so mostly he let me be.

When Dunbar was young, we called him our "blue collar worker." He seemed to love to dig, but luckily only where we encouraged him to. When we purchased the house in Cambridge and decided to put drainage pipe in the basement, Dunbar did some of the digging. We were installing it in an area where it was difficult for someone of our height to dig. We would point to an area where we wanted to install the pipe and say, "Dig." He would dig with wild abandon. When we wanted to add a pool to our property and there was an old cherry tree growing in the precise spot where we needed to dig, we pointed and said "Dig" and he would dig with joyous zeal.

Murphy of the "semi-precious stone," story, along with Raven, became part of our family before I became ill. When Murphy (named for an Irish beer I tended to prefer to Guinness in those Irish pubs) was a young dog, she would go to work with me and accompany me while I planted flowers. I took her kennel with me to keep her in when I worked, so she would begin *wanting* to be nearby. She could stay there in it, playing or napping, but always staying with me, keeping me company. I never got to spend time with her later. She had gone to live with my brother's family before I came home.

Raven was an adorable, if a little crazy, girl who loved to play ball. She was truly a lab and would chase and retrieve any ball or stick or whatever you could throw, longer than you could throw it.

She was our only bitch. Our house was usually full to overflowing with testosterone. Raven was the most difficult dog to train. A local dog trainer suggested staring her down to establish dominance. We could then more easily train her. I thought, "I can do that."

At that time, if I was going to be talking for a long time on the telephone, I was in the habit of sinking down to the floor under the phone to rest. Also, at that time, Raven, at only about twelve weeks, could still be easily handled. I was trying to "multi-task." I picked her up and holding her in what I thought was the proper position, turned her around so that we were nose to nose. In that way, I could "stare her down." She reached out and bit my lip! When I screeched, my cover was blown and the person I was talking with on the phone knew I wasn't concentrating on the conversation alone!

Even with her wild side, she seemed to sense my need for comfort and was a good companion to me in her quieter moments. Unfortunately, the pompom on my hat looked like a ball to her making car trips "fascinating."

Jasper, another black lab, came to live with us when he was eighteen months old. He had been well-trained in the "Guiding Eyes for the Blind" program, but he was released before the second phase of the training because he was apparently too gentle. The trainers were concerned that, because of Jasper's gentle nature, he would not make good decisions. They feared he would try to please and might lead someone into traffic if they told him to cross a street, rather than deny him or her.

The program coordinator thought Jasper would be great around a wheelchair, so she contacted Jim. We thought we would be on a waiting list for years, so this was a great surprise! We already had Raven as a part of our "family," and we really didn't know how she would feel about sharing her territory. At first, though, Raven paid little attention to Jasper. When she went with us to meet him, she ignored him and just kept playing with her ball. Later they became friends, but Jasper, always the gentleman, deferred to whatever Raven wanted.

As time passed, it became apparent that Jasper had an eyesight problem himself. He sometimes barked at my husband or my father until they came close enough that he could recognize them. (I think my wheelchair, perhaps, kept him from barking at me!)

Although he was very much Jim's dog -- depending on him for important things like, "Who will feed me?" and "Who will walk me?" -- He decided he would protect me.

The first time we came in from the garden together at my parents' house, I was pushing myself backwards up the ramp to go into the house. (Pushing is easier than pulling, but it isn't easy to see what is behind you!) I didn't know at the time, but my mother, who was watching at the door, told me later that Jasper walked behind me. He would sit and wait for me to reach him; then he would continue up the ramp and wait for me to reach him again.

One very hot day, we took Jasper and Raven to a nearby pond so they could go for a swim and cool down. Jasper, being a good, strong swimmer, would swim out and retrieve the stick that Jim would throw. Raven would "allow" Jasper to fetch the stick. Jasper would swim back to shore and drop the stick while he shook the water off. Raven would then move in, retrieve the stick and wait for the accolades!

Even though we fed him only expensive low calorie food, Jasper weighed in at 120 pounds. We also fed him carrots as a reward (Not just *any* carrots. He preferred the more expensive baby carrots to regular carrots cut into sticks, so that's what he got.) He didn't move much, so he didn't expend much energy.

His favorite thing to do was to sleep in the shower at our home in Cambridge. Whenever we came home with him after being gone, he would head straight for his special place in the shower. We could find him there day or night when we were home.

This was never really a problem for us, except when we hosted my brother's wedding. We forgot to post a sign and one guest said they heard snoring coming from the shower and thought it might be someone who had had a really good time at the reception and was "sleeping it off." She pulled back the shower curtain to reveal Jasper!

His massive size earned him the nick-name "The Big Woof" from some of our little cousins. We, however, called him our "Gentle Giant." He had such kind, expressive eyes.

With all the training and obedience classes he'd had, as well as the exposure to different people and situations, Jim and I decided he would make a good therapy dog, visiting people in hospitals and rehabs. His main job would be just to make people smile -- maybe to help them remember a dog they had known. He began his visitations.

With his status as a registered therapy dog to credit him, he for a while, also went with me to my horticultural therapy sessions in Ballston Spa.

Jasper loved the attention he received from the local high school kids who attended special classes there almost as much as he loved the carrots that I took along for his treats.

Sometimes, given his "lay-about" nature, even this seemed a little too taxing for him. Jim and I didn't give up on him, though, and Jasper eventually found his niche.

The therapy dog group we were affiliated with supported a program whereby school-age children read to dogs. This seemed to help with the children's reading skills because the dogs don't judge them -- dogs don't care if children don't pronounce something correctly. It seemed to be a perfect job for Jasper.

In the past, we had noticed that if Jasper wasn't the center of attention, he would bark until he got that attention. That was not a good trait for a therapy dog to have! In this case, he could just lie there, do nothing but relax, and get the attention he so craved. It seemed to be a perfect job for him, and the children who read to him did improve their reading skills.

Jasper retired when his age and health made visiting children too difficult. Everyone he met loved him. It was a very sad day when he passed away.

Chapter 9

Outpatient Therapy

In an effort to get stronger and remain nimble after I returned home, I began doing calisthenics for an hour every day that I was at my parents' house in Salem. I was not as dedicated at home in Cambridge. There are so many things that I want to, or feel I *need* to, accomplish when I'm there. When I could ignore the gardening -- itself a great physical activity -- I did walk with Jim's assistance on a treadmill, and later rode a stationary recumbent bicycle. Also, I continued my therapy on an outpatient basis at Wesley, which included physical, occupational and speech therapy.

I remember two outpatient occupational therapists from Wesley quite well: Christie and Ceil.

Christie, I remember, was expecting twins. Her husband worked for the company that makes

Mars Bars. I was pretty impressed by that. She was a young, enthusiastic woman who tuned in to my needs and helped me have a little fun with my therapy.

Ceil was so much fun -- entertaining. I knew her therapy was going to be eventful! Ceil was the one who taught me "righty/tighty, lefty/loosey." I had never heard that saying before. Another automatic thing that was simply "gone." I couldn't, for the life of me, remember how to screw or unscrew a cap. It made applying face cream quite difficult and opening toothpaste impossible. The top was also very small on the toothpaste, and I just could not turn it (finally, we found flip tops.)

Ceil's words stayed with me for a long time. They are something I find myself repeating, even today, when I use anything involving a lid. It is like a song you can't forget, though you try: "righty/tighty, lefty/loosey."

Michelle was a physical therapist who understood where I was coming from more than most, because her husband had been in a car accident. She knew my frustrations because she had seen these challenges before. However, that didn't mean that she was "easy" on me. We used to walk with the walker and she could always convince me to take a few extra steps when I thought I was tired.

Michelle and I frequently worked in the pool, but I did not want to put my face in the water for a long while. It might have been that the rhythmic breathing, necessary for swimming, bothered me. I had a really hard time coping with anything that could "control" me, and breathing in water *is* a real possibility if you forget to breathe properly.

That was another thing that was hard to believe. I had always enjoyed swimming and had been a strong swimmer. It had been automatic and natural. I grew up swimming in my parents' pool. After my AVM, swimming seemed monumentally difficult. It took an immense amount of concentration to coordinate all those movements.

One day, Michelle requested that I perform the backstroke. Jim was watching and taping, so that we could show it to my parents later. When I finished my backstroke laps, Jim said, "That was great! Now, take a bow!" I of course, didn't think, bent from the waist, bowed and put my face right in the four-foot deep water. Perfect! The problem that I had with putting my face in the water was solved!

From then on, Michelle and I worked on the breaststroke and the crawl. It has been like that all through my entire recovery. Each success was built upon another. There is no quick and easy solution to a stroke.

Since having the AVM, changes have depended upon me "getting" something else; accomplishing something before moving on to a new challenge. I have found patience that I did not know that I possess. I never dreamed that I would have to re-learn so many things. I found I had to invent a different way altogether of doing some things.

The swimming sessions with Michelle happened soon after I went home to live. At that time, on the nights that I stayed at my parents' house, Mom and I were sleeping downstairs on a sofa bed. My parents didn't feel comfortable with me sleeping alone yet. I can understand that, I suppose. They were unsure of my breathing.

As it turned out, it was later decided that I should use an air machine (C-PAP) at night because my breathing was so irregular. I would take a few breaths and then just not breathe for a few seconds. For a time, I slept in a reclined chair to help me breathe -- to try to prevent the gaps in my breathing. The chair was placed beside Mom's bed so she could be sure I was breathing. She told me that she listened to my breathing patterns at night then.

I can still hear Dad ask, "How many eyes were watching you in the night?" He was, of course, referring to Mom and the dog (Raven) staring at me while I slept. I'm sure that Mom was checking on my safety and Raven just wanted to play ball. It was a bit unnerving to realize you were being watched, though.

In the middle of the night one night, Mom woke me and asked, "What are you doing?" "The backstroke" was my reply.

I guess I was talking -- and swimming -- in my sleep, because the following day I recalled none of it. I laugh about it now, because it *does* remind me of the old joke, "Waiter, what's this fly doing in my soup?" The waiter looks at the fly and says, "The backstroke!" At least, it all demonstrated how serious I was about my swimming exercises -- even thinking about them in my sleep!

Judy, who was my age and liked music as much as I did, became my physical therapist after Michelle. We used to sing with the radio as I swam laps in the pool or exercised in the therapy room. The singing helped keep my mind off what I was doing, and as a result my swimming became more natural. I also didn't realize that I was working so hard.

Judy was a lot of fun, which was exactly what I needed at the time. She convinced me to work hard without my realizing what I was doing. My muscles really got a work-out on the days when I exercised with her!

She motivated me in PT and really pushed me to do more than I thought I could possibly do. She also took an interest in what I was doing at home and gave me some good ideas of things to try. Her suggestions gave me incentive to intensify my home exercise program.

Judy also visited me and took me for rides in her car...on "field trips." What a feeling that was! I was doing something "normal" again.

Once, we went to a park in Saratoga where I met a little boy who asked about my wheelchair. I made a joke about it to answer his question, but I remember promising myself then that I wasn't going to be sitting in it forever.

I was also going to a horticultural therapy program in Ballston Spa, New York, which was offered by the Cornell Co-operative Extension (the county agricultural department). It gave me the chance to do something I love instead of something I had to do to get better.

In our planting, we were using soilless mix and not "dirt." As one of my college professors maintained, "Dirt is something you sweep under the rug," he said. "What you grow plants in is soil, or soilless mix." The mix contained peat moss, mostly from Canadian bogs -- perlite which looks like a little pearl, and vermiculite; shiny and gold-colored. When these things are combined, and especially when mixed with water, they create a unique odor that I instantly recognized.

They say that the olfactory sense is the strongest sense. I can certainly attest to that. I breathed in deeply and was taken back to my "pre-AVM" life. One of my favorite things to do was to walk out at night to my greenhouses in the field behind our house. (It was especially nice to crunch through fresh snow to get there.) After turning on the lights, I would breathe in the rich, soil-scented air and take a moment to enjoy the peace and quiet before checking my plants and the greenhouse heaters.

Sinking my hands into the earthy mix that day in Ballston, I shared my thoughts with Carol, my therapist. The memories were strong -- intense -- almost overpowering. I longed to get back to my greenhouses and I wondered if I ever would. At the same time, I was happy to be working with plants again, and I still enjoy my work at Ballston.

Chapter 10

Losing Time Again

Once, when I was riding in the car with my parents near Rutland, Vermont, we stopped at a greenhouse. People came to the car to greet me. I didn't recall having met them before, but I suddenly remembered that their greenhouse lost an entire truckload of Easter lilies. They froze on their way to market in Boston. The lady who owned the business had been a nurse in the rehabilitation center in Rutland where I had been a patient for a short time. That was obviously very important to me because of what I did for a living before the AVM and therefore I remembered it.

As a wholesale greenhouse owner, I grew assorted flowers; thousands of geraniums in every hue imaginable; New Guinea impatiens, tuberous begonias, assorted hanging baskets, vinca vine and dracaena, and packs of flowers. I also grew chrysanthemums and ornamental cabbage and kale for planting in the fall and to be sold wholesale.

During the summer, I planted gardens and maintained them for people in Manchester, Vermont, who were mainly summer residents there. I felt that if I worked very hard, the business would be a success. I think that is one of the reasons my recovery has seemed so laborious. I feel that I have been working very hard to return to being the person that I was before my illness, and I just haven't seen the results I thought I should.

When I was still living in Wesley, I remember lying in bed and thinking I would resume my work in Manchester. I thought that climbing up on the back deck of condominiums to care for planters would be difficult because of the stairs, but I could surely do the rest of the job. Hefting the watering can to tend the plants would not be problematic, I thought, even if I couldn't lift heavy things. Cleaning off flowers that were no longer in their prime wouldn't be a problem, even if I could not manipulate my fingers and make them "pinch" the plants. I kept thinking, "Tomorrow, I'll be better." That "tomorrow" hasn't come yet.

It is true that an overnight recovery only happens in the movies.

I have certainly hit peaks and valleys, and I have come across plateaus several times in the last few years. Every time that I hit a plateau, I felt as if I was spinning my wheels and couldn't make myself take off again. When it seemed most hopeless and I didn't have the strength to keep trying, Jim would tell me, "If you work hard and keep trying, there are no guarantees that you'll get better, but if you don't try, I can guarantee that you won't."

I usually think of the things I cannot do, instead of what I *can* do. I need to have someone point out what I can accomplish and what I *have* accomplished. At numerous times during the recovery process, we *all* (my entire family) needed to hear that it "can be done."

I always did my best work whenever I heard, "it can't be done." Jim said he noticed that as well. He would say "game face" and I would always work a bit harder to do really difficult (well, taxing anyway) exercises. To my knowledge, I had never heard the phrase before, but I somehow knew what Jim meant when he said, "GAME FACE." I would grit my teeth and finish some task. After I finished one difficult exercise, I would do another, even when we all thought that I had no strength left. It seems like I just have to be "challenged."

I really disliked that word when I attended Cornell, where we were quite regularly "challenged," but somehow it sounds "right" now. Bit by bit, I am still getting better. It is simply not in me to totally give up. The encouragement I have received from family and friends has been so helpful.

Right now, I need so much help, even for something as basic as going somewhere. I am still not able to drive a car, and there is no such thing as mass transit in the little town I live in, so I have to depend on someone to take me everywhere I want or need to go. I am definitely not used to that.

After I went home, Tammi, my guardian angel from Wesley, and I became friends, as well as patient/therapist. She was great at getting me out of the house. We would go shopping together or have dinner and see a movie. That probably did more for me than a therapy session could do. I felt "normal" for a few hours. I was busy doing something that anyone else might do. It didn't matter that I was in a wheelchair.

Tammi even went to Myrtle Beach with us a couple of times. We all rode down in our motorhome. Jim and I stayed in it near the beach while Tammi and my parents stayed in a nearby condominium.

The motorhome is something that we purchased post-AVM. Jim and I always liked to travel, but traveling in the motorhome took the place of the car or flying. Taking "our home" with us made the most sense. Since I was in a wheelchair, tenting wasn't an option (we tried it without great success), and I was apprehensive about flying because of my shunt, even though a doctor that I checked with said it would be "okay." I certainly did not want to have a headache like the one I had experienced with the AVM, ever again.

Each time we traveled to Myrtle Beach, we had a wonderful week full of sun, shopping and eating too much. It was a nice and restful vacation for everyone. Jim was able to take a well-deserved break and even golfed with an uncle who was also vacationing there.

While at Myrtle Beach, I walked for the first time in a long time. Supported between Jim and Tammi, who held my arms to help me remain upright and keep my balance, I got up on my feet. It was hard work, harder than I remembered certainly, but I walked! I am sure the sand hampered my progress, but it was also much more forgiving than asphalt would have been. I can't begin to describe the feeling that I had. I felt so good that I bent down to pick up a couple of shells -- not even beautiful shells -- it was a big deal for me to be able to do that, though, and I will always remember it.

We don't think about the freedom that walking allows us until it's not there. It is something that we automatically do, not something that we have to concentrate on, or even think briefly about. You just quickly get on your feet and put one foot in front of the other. Easy. I know that I took it for granted before the AVM.

Before the AVM, I took my independence for granted, as well. I am still discovering just how independent I was. I did what I wanted, when I wanted to do it. I have to rely on someone else for almost everything now -- on their schedule.

This is a decidedly difficult thing for me -- to admit that I need help and then to ask for it -- but I know it's the way things must be now.

Four years after I left Wesley to make our house "home" once again, I had achieved a different kind of balance. I was still pushing myself to improve, but I was also working with what I could do. There was even some talk of me working in a local hardware store as they considered opening a gardening section.

At the time, I was taking larger doses of valproic acid than those that I am currently taking. Valproic acid is supposed to prevent more seizures. These seizures may have been caused by the original bleed or by scarring from the surgery to remove the AVM.

Most medications do have side effects and display different ones in different people. In my case the medication caused unimaginable fatigue. Fatigue *is* a side effect, or an adverse effect of the medication.

I despised that tired feeling that I got and considered it my biggest problem. I knew I had once been energetic and I found it exceedingly perplexing and annoying that I couldn't regain that. My limbs would feel leaden, and I would feel completely drained. Sometimes, I would fall asleep without even knowing it was coming. One minute, I would be awake and talking, completely aware of my surroundings, then I would be fast asleep while sitting up in my chair. It would sometimes even happen while I was at the dinner table. It was quite embarrassing.

It seemed to be worth it to eliminate the valproic acid and see if that was the problem and so, during one of our appointments, I talked to my neurologist about stopping the medication. Since I had not had a seizure in a number of years, he thought it was it a good step, and advised cutting back my dosage over a period of time.

My neurologist also gave me the okay for a few "sips" of beer. You are not supposed to drink alcoholic beverages while taking valproic acid. I just wanted to be able to have a glass of champagne at a wedding or a beer with a piece of pizza without worrying about the medication interacting with alcohol.

After that appointment, we celebrated by stopping at a local brewpub for lunch, and I ordered the first beer I had had in years. It made me rather nervous to hold a glass near my teeth and my hands shook too much to tip the glass, so I had to drink with a straw. It tasted the same as I remembered, though. Another step in my recovery! The celebrating was short-lived.

We discovered later that the valproic acid had apparently helped with other problems. After stopping the medication completely, I started "losing time" again. It was a gradual thing and went on for several months until it was finally realized that my problems coincided with stopping the medication. My aunt Jackie, who is a nurse, brought that to my mother's attention.

Mom first noticed that something was wrong with me when my short-term memory problems became acute. Also, she was having difficulty getting my attention. She would say my name several times with no response from me. Finally, she would raise her voice, calling my name, and I would be startled and then respond.

At that same time, Judy, the physical therapist who I was seeing at Wesley, also told Mom that "things seemed to start happening when she (I) stopped taking the seizure medication." She observed that I gradually became "different." She noticed the changes in me -- in my personality and overall ability and willingness to concentrate and cooperate in therapy sessions.

Jim, Dad and Mom have a hard time talking about the second period of time that I don't remember -- the period of time when I was cutting back on, or had stopped taking my medication. When I learned of some of my actions during that time, they made no sense to me. The person that I was does not sound like me at all. I probably would not even like that person! It is, therefore, a bit difficult to hear about her.

Have you ever dozed off while riding in a car and then suddenly snapped awake? A different song is playing on the radio and conversations around you have skipped to new topics. When you look out the window, you see strange scenery passing you by and it takes a moment to figure out where you are. You stretch and yawn and ask, "How long have I been asleep?"

Imagine how you'd feel if your fellow passengers said, "You were asleep? We didn't know. You've been talking the whole time."

Imagine how I felt when I found out that, not only had I been "napping," but while I was "out," I had been replaced by an imposter who said and did some very strange things that left my family bewildered, upset and exhausted.

The "imposter" became obsessed with several things during that shadow time, and my behavior became so erratic that my parents were concerned for my safety. If I was going for a ride in my parents' car, I would lock and unlock all the doors. Then I would use the electronic controls to work all the windows, and I sometimes would unbuckle my seat belt. I would also, once in a while, open my door a bit. I am sure that it was very annoying to everyone around me, but it was as if I was forced to do it. It had no meaning to me. I believe the injury to my brain manifested itself in *meaningless obsessions.*

I suddenly developed an obsession with paper, and I simply had to have it. Wherever I was -- a doctor's waiting room or any other place I had to wait -- I tore pages out of magazines to use when I was in the loo. Mom told me she didn't know why I did that. They certainly did not restrict bathroom tissue. I never used it for anything. I just had to have paper. My doctor says this is called "obsessive compulsive" behavior.

Once, at my neuropsychologist's office, Jim returned to the waiting area from talking alone with my doctor in her office, and found me stuffing my sleeves, my pants and shoes with papers, while the receptionist, who thought it was "cute," laughed and laughed at my antics.

Mom said that they always had to check me whenever I came home from any waiting area, because I would stuff the pages that I had pilfered wherever I could. They would find the folded pages in my pockets, stuffed in my sleeves, as padding in my shoulders, and in my shoes. I was very resourceful and found numerous hiding spots. Jim, who tried to have a sense of humor about it all, told me that they always had to "pat me down" after an appointment.

I do remember some of that time, I guess. I just don't remember all of it, or even much of it. That is probably a good thing. I have often felt that while my brain was healing, it protected me from things that would have been difficult to hear, and, therefore, maybe even detrimental to my getting better.

I know that I also became obsessive over being in the bathroom. I am told I was asking to use the bathroom literally every five minutes, and we tried different methods so that I could "adjust" my thought processes. We would set an alarm clock for every two hours at first. We then had a schedule that was posted on the bathroom door on which I would check off the time. I don't remember doing those things.

At one point, every time I got in the car, I asked if we were going right home, or if we had to stop someplace on the way home. The reason for this was so that I could figure out where the nearest bathroom was and how it was set up in case I needed one. Was I familiar with it? The Americans With Disabilities Act ensured that I would have ready access to a bathroom. I have, however, been in bathrooms that were difficult, if not impossible, to negotiate, especially with my ataxia and lack of balance. Those bathrooms were, most definitely, not designed by someone in a wheelchair!

From morning until night, I was thinking about the next time I would need the loo. I realized that I would have to "go" first thing in the morning, so I tried to remember to put my slippers right beside the bed at night. Then I could reach them and put them on while Mom or Jim was busy doing other things, such as opening the curtains and putting the shades up. I would be ready.

Jim did tell me that I was catheterized for so long that I might not have "normal" sensations. Sometimes when I got into the bathroom, I had no or very little results. I had to accept that because of my short-term memory problems, I would forget that I had already "gone" a short time before. If I didn't write down when I had been in the loo, I couldn't remember if I should go. I started carrying a piece of paper with me so I could note the time of my bathroom visits. This was in addition to the posted record. I also had to write down the time when I exercised because, if I didn't, I quite often didn't remember the time I should stop.

The "timing" worked out quite well for a while and gave me some structure even though it seemed that I always was in need of the loo before the scheduled time. After starting medicine for overactive bladder, it wasn't unusual for me to feel that I could postpone beyond the scheduled time. Sometimes, I would go for a *much* longer time, which helped everyone sleep a bit more.

There are a few times that are quite pronounced in my memory. Times when I felt that I could have "gone" before the designated time. One occurred when I went out to dinner in Saratoga with my parents. In the short car ride from the mall where we were shopping, to a restaurant approximately fifteen minutes later, I felt the "urge" again.

I had "gone" before we left the mall, but I truly felt "in need" again. I ordered my dinner and struggled through the meal but I was really very uncomfortable. We did eventually use the loo before leaving the restaurant. Although I thought I could have used it before my meal arrived, I realize now that my parents were just trying to help get me back on track.

Because I was in the wheelchair, which gave me some mobility, I could have found a loo earlier, but that simply did not occur to me. I believe that, at the time, I wasn't thinking for myself much. I was quite used to having someone else make decisions for me. (My neuropsychologist eventually advised Mom that enough time had passed and I should be able to handle those trips myself. I wouldn't have to wait if the time wasn't right.)

To add to all of this drama, at one point, I had a serious bladder infection and was taken to the hospital in an ambulance that pulled up to my parents' front door to get me. Apparently, I developed a high temperature in a short period of time and even began to hallucinate, frightening everyone. It seems that I have a history of bladder infections, but usually not that severe.

Throughout this strange and disturbing set of circumstances, Jim and my parents were constantly in touch with my neurologist, my neuropsychologist and other doctors as they tried to figure out the cause of all of my strange behaviors and medical problems.

Seven years after having the AVM, and almost five years after I had been living at home, my father took me to a nearby city for an MRI. Everyone wanted to be certain that the health concerns I was having were because I had decreased my medication, and not because of any other medical factor; that there was nothing happening with my brain.

I have no memory of a great deal of that time, but I do remember that test. Luckily, I was not prone to claustrophobia, although I did understand how being in that machine could be difficult for some people. While I was inside it, I found that closing my eyes was quite helpful, as the tube was only inches from my face. What really was difficult for me, though, was the incessant, loud clicking noise I heard. I thought that listening to music would have helped -- a little Van Morrison singing about Tupelo Honey, perhaps. I wished, at the time, that someone had suggested it to me.

It helped to know that Dad was inches away -- just outside that cold, gray cylinder. He talked to me, reminded me to "lie completely still," and held my hand throughout the entire test.

Dad took the result of the test to Dr. Jenkyn, my doctor at Dartmouth, catching him as he was leaving for the day. He asked Dad to wait a minute while he put his things in his car. He went back inside with Dad, and put a picture of my brain up where they could view it together. He then said, "The brain appears normal. Meg won't be having any more problems with that. There is nothing wrong with it."

Even though I had what was termed a "normal MRI," I was still having memory and sleeping problems in addition to my compulsive and erratic behavior, so I continued to see my neuropsychologist throughout the fall and winter of that year. That winter, I was returned to Dartmouth for testing. Based on those tests and follow-up appointments and because of my erratic behavior, I was put back on the valproic acid, which seemed to help my behavior. I was, however, given a much lower dosage than I originally was taking.

Going off my meds should never have had the effect that it did have. It was not predicted, but then, it seems that I was never "predictable." One of my therapists always said that I "never was a textbook case." I still needed some medication, just not as much. Other case studies have since indicated that valproic acid regulates more than just seizure activity. In all probability, I will be taking that medication for the rest of my life.

Chapter 11

Moving On

It is difficult to describe my feelings when I realized that I had once again "lost time." I tried not to dwell on it. I tried not to think about it at all at first, because I honestly did not understand it all, and I was hoping that time would make it clearer. Well, it didn't.

One night when Dad and I were watching the Notre Dame football game together (they won 21 -14) he said I should "forget" the last year because it had been so difficult. I found that very interesting. What did I have to "forget?" I had no idea that something had been wrong -- that I hadn't acted "right" for a while. It is strange to me that I could be participating in everyday activities and be so unaware of them.

It bothers me that everyone seemed to know what was happening to me, except me. There were quite a few things that I remembered absolutely nothing about, and I wanted to know about everything.

Tammi, my friend and physical therapist from Wesley, seemed to know that I may have been having small seizures. I didn't seem "right." She also told me that I wasn't very nice to my parents at that time: that I got a bit "outspoken." I, of course, don't remember it.

Jim also said that I may have been having small seizures, and the seizures may have erased my memory. He added that I acted towards him the same "rotten" way that I was treating my parents. This cannot have been much fun for anyone.

Janet, my Speech Therapist, drew up a timeline for me that said I became a patient at Wesley in Saratoga Springs in June. I went home and began outpatient therapy in September the following year. At that time, I began going to speech class once per week, instead of the three times per week I had "Speech" when I lived at Wesley. I later "graduated" from Speech Therapy, but I began again after a re-evaluation indicated that I had gotten "sloppy" with my speech, and I was in need of a refresher course. I wasn't participating in speech therapy for fifteen months, and I did not remember those months at all. That was a long time that passed me by that I was not cognizant of.

It was fortunate that I saw Janet's timeline. When Mom and I looked at it together, I suddenly realized that I had lost not just a little time again, but months! "The penny dropped" once again.

Everything that I thought had taken place in the current year had, in reality, happened the year before. It's still so unreal and feels incredibly strange. I didn't discover many things until sometime later when somebody would tell me what had occurred -- our President had been in office longer than I thought, for example. My understanding of what had happened was all still evolving. I was still not certain of exactly when I started "losing time" again.

A few months after I began medicating with valproic acid again, I started keeping my own journal. My first entry was a lengthy one in which I truly sound like that passenger in the car who just woke up.

In it, I noted that, "Yesterday, Mary was here to exercise for the last time." We'd been meeting once a week but I can only remember the last two times. What a strange feeling to know someone was here, and not be able to remember it.

I also noted "Mary was my first Physical Therapist at Wesley, and through a mutual friend, actually got me into Wesley, where beds are at a premium." I thought it was odd. My parents seemed to know her before I was admitted, but she was a stranger to me. If she was such an important part of my life, how then could they know her when I did not?

Something that really bothered me during my second recovery was that I couldn't remember the ring that was on my hand next to my wedding band. It was, of course, my engagement ring and yet it wasn't. I didn't recognize it... it didn't look familiar at all. It most definitely was not the engagement ring that I remembered.

I asked Mom about it one day when I was getting ready for pool therapy. She looked at me closely, and asked, "Don't you remember what happened to your engagement ring?" As I thought about it, I suddenly remembered it like it had just happened. The "penny dropped" again! It was as if someone had punched me in the stomach, doubling me over.

I could picture the original setting and the setting with the stone missing. The diamond had fallen out of it and was gone for good even though everyone searched for it. I felt so terrible the first time that I remembered it...how could I not even know where, or when, I had lost it? I could have lost it at Wesley -- in the pool or on a mat, at home in Cambridge, or in Salem on the floor where I was exercising or in bed when I was sleeping. I had no idea where it was.

My new ring has three diamonds in it -- for past, present and future. It is an anniversary ring and it is beautiful, but I didn't recognize it. Jim bought it for me to replace the lost diamond. One mystery solved! I really wish all the mysteries could be that easily explained.

The more I thought about that ring, though, the worse I felt because I had asked Jim so many times about the ring and where it had come from. I was sad that I didn't remember him giving it to me. What other important and special moments were missing from my memory?

I talked with Helen, another college buddy, on the phone one night and she told me about the time she and her family came to visit and stayed at a local Bed and Breakfast. They had visited before and stayed in our house in Cambridge, but I had no idea that they had visited a second time. I guess it was during the second period of time when I just wasn't remembering things. We will probably never know for certain what happened to me medically during that time, although my neurologist, Dr. Jenkyn, did enlighten me as to what *may* have occurred with the absence of my medication. Stopping my meds could "certainly be associated with increased symptoms." He also said that the "behavioral traits that have become magnified are due to [my] brain injury."

One autumn day, I was outside in Salem, using the standing bar on the porch. (The "standing bar" is a horizontal hand rail, attached at both ends that I use for support and for balance. I can grab the bar when I lose my balance.) On that day, I was wearing a purple wool jacket that I did not remember owning. Dad said that he had bought it for me the year before at Eastern States Exposition in Massachusetts and had given it to me for Christmas. The jacket seemed brand new to me, so I thanked him for it.

Another day when I went out to the standing bar, I had on another coat that I didn't remember. Did I borrow it from my mother? It was a pretty, powder blue down coat that my parents also gave me for Christmas that year. It feels very strange to wear clothes that I cannot remember. It makes me wonder about my reaction when I received them. Was I thankful enough? What did I say?

My short-term memory problems can be extremely annoying. Mom had to explain several times in one day what I had given Tammi for Christmas during my second loss of time. I could *not* remember some things. From one moment to the next, I would forget. Actually, it was from one second to the next! (The gift was a little figurine that somehow had a special meaning. I just couldn't remember what that meaning was.)

We met Tammi for some shopping, and we saw an identical figurine on display in one of the stores we visited. She exclaimed over it, and I didn't tell her at the time that I didn't remember it. I should have known that she would understand. (I later talked with Tammi on the phone and she did understand, of course.)

I felt so confused. I quite often thought of studying at Cornell, and of how I could no longer attempt such a thing. That made me extremely angry. The hills of Ithaca would not have been kind to a wheelchair. I would have loved to have been able to take some classes to fill my days, but, I thought, my memory problems would make it impossible, even if the logistics could be dealt with through the use of a computer.

I still yearn to know exactly how much time I lost that time. I discovered that we went to

Pennsylvania instead of Myrtle Beach when I noticed a plaque hanging on the inside of our front door in Cambridge that I hadn't remembered seeing before. The plaque is a snowman with "Winter Greetings" written on it. Jim said that he bought it for me on that trip to Pennsylvania, and he gave it to me for Christmas...all a mystery to me! I didn't remember the trip, or that particular Christmas.

Even now, it is such a strange and unsettling feeling to realize that the trip to Myrtle Beach that I was thinking of had been two years earlier than I remembered. Even worse, I was told that I had been so "difficult" that Jim and I couldn't take a long-planned vacation to the Grand Canyon, because I was "such a handful" and wouldn't sit still in the motorhome. Jim couldn't be certain of my behavior.

I talked to Jim one night and when I mentioned it, he reminded me that we went as far west as Indiana and visited his nephew, his nephew's wife and baby. After he mentioned it, the incident did sound somewhat familiar. I vaguely remembered being in Indiana, but I had no idea we had planned to go on to the Grand Canyon.

Apparently, I was going through the motions of daily life, but didn't really know what was going on around me. I want to put that dark time behind me, but I also want to know that everything is all right now -- that I won't have a problem again.

Throughout my recovery, I have had trouble sleeping well, and I went to a sleep lab in Saratoga and to another at Dartmouth's hospital eighteen months later. Apparently, I was keeping everyone awake at home, because I was so restless. The tests were run as "a last resort" to solve our nighttime dilemma. Both labs were controlled environments run by technicians and I was supposed to perform by sleeping. Sounded easy.

The doctors at Dartmouth confirmed what the one in Saratoga had diagnosed. I had sleep apnea and needed additional air at night. I don't remember being at Dartmouth, but I *do* remember the lab in Saratoga. I sat up straight in bed most of the time. I was quite restless. The next morning, the person running the lab asked Jim if I was like that every night. Jim just said, "Yes." The technician was extremely sympathetic to Jim's plight.

So many nights Mom tells me, "Lie still." That sounds to me like it is somehow my fault that I am not sleeping. Her explanation is if I don't lie still, my body will never relax enough to go to sleep. This makes me very angry and sad, because I know that even if that makes perfect sense, I am not doing it on purpose. I also know I am not going to feel very well the day after I cannot sleep and I do *try* to sleep. I *want* to.

It seems like the less I sleep, the worse my memory becomes. It really bothers me that I have such a bad memory. I remember some things just fine and not others. I really don't know why some things stick in my mind and others do not.

Jim and I have come up with all kinds of memory devises for me to use, because I still need to associate things somehow. For example, today is Tuesday, so I think of Wimpy's phrase, "I'll gladly pay you Tuesday (or was it 'dues day'?) for a hamburger today." Why that sticks with me, I don't know, but phrases such as this help me remember.

During September and October, I was still having a bit of difficulty falling asleep, and I felt nervous that something was going to happen again. I wondered if I would always feel that way. Would I always be ready to quickly blame everything on my AVM and the possibility of having seizures? Mom said nothing was going to happen to me, but that "those problems are all in the past," but I was still concerned.

One night, Mom finally had to get up and give me a PM (pill) just so that I could relax enough to fall asleep. Then, I slept very soundly until 7:00 a.m. without even getting up to use the loo in the night! It was so good to wake up and look at my watch and realize that I had slept so long. What a wonderful feeling!

I wrote (entered in my computer) quite often during that fall and had some good days that I'm glad I recorded. It's nice to be able to look back and remind myself of the good things that happened.

On September 3rd, I wrote that I had remembered the day and date for the first time without prompting or looking in the newspaper. That had become a big deal with me, and several times a day, I would look it up or ask Jim or my parents. Remembering it myself was pretty important to me.

The next day was important, as well. I wrote: "I walked today! Judy walked in front of me in the parallel bars and gave me voice commands." I can still hear "squeeze the left cheek, weight off the right side, swing the right foot, and land on the heel." We walked between the parallel bars, Judy walking backwards, watching me and talking to me; urging me on, and with me slowly walking toward her. So I would feel more secure, we walked between the parallel bars so I could grab the bars if I stumbled, which didn't happen much. Boy, did it feel good to walk! It had been eight years of sitting in a bed or wheelchair.

Mom saw it and was so happy for me. She had me tell Carol at Ballston where I was having horticultural therapy. I slept all the way home in the car. Soundly for almost an hour. I was exhausted.

When Aunt Barbara and Uncle Jack walked to our house in the evening, I told them. They were very happy for me, too. Everyone knew it was a major accomplishment for me.

September 8th was an especially good day for me, as well. Jim and I spent the day at our home in Cambridge and I wrote: "90's today -- very nice! Jim and I exercised out on the lawn and then made stuffed zucchini together for dinner. He said, it was 'just like old times'! We used to cook together a lot." Spending a normal day with my husband is something I have always appreciated, but I have learned to never take it for granted.

Considering my problems with sleeping and going to the loo, which seem to be so interconnected, my journal entry on September 16th was also pretty satisfying. "Slept great last night," I typed. "It was good to wake up so refreshed. I took a PM again and it worked great. I feel like I should do an advertisement! I slept from midnight to 4:00 am. (I started taking Ditropan for overactive bladder and I think it finally became effective in the last few days. Now, I don't need to get up so much and pee, so dozing off is not a problem.)

On October 3rd, I was staying with my parents in Salem and I wrote that my father and I took the scooter out. Sometimes, Mom and I take the scooter out, but usually I go with Dad. It really isn't easy with two women under one roof, and after a few days together, Mom and I tend to get on each other's nerves. To get me out of the house and give my mother a "breather," my father and I take a trip through town while he tells me histories of the town. It's been fun, because we've "gone inside" some houses and "met" the people that lived there when Dad and Mom were in high school.

By November, I felt that I was on my way again. I had that good feeling that you have when you feel like you are accomplishing something. I was sort of pleased with myself, and with what I was doing. I could not wait to get downstairs in the morning. I would lie in bed and think about what I was going to do that day. I might read a book, work on the computer, write a cookbook index (for recipes that I compiled) on the laptop, or clean house if I was stuck inside.

If the weather cooperated and I went outside at home, I could take Jasper, our dog at that time, for a run with the golf cart. My family contributed toward the purchase of my cart, which allows me to see parts of my property I would otherwise not be able to visit.

With the golf cart, Jasper and I (with the dog running along beside me because I could never convince Jasper to ride on the seat with me) would go out on "inspection tours" in the morning and compile a list of things that Jim *"might want to do."*

I had a great day in physical therapy near the end of that November. I walked with Judy and finally I felt good again. For a while, the motions of walking would not come to me and I had to wait for that time to pass. When I tried to walk, I felt like my hands were pulling me off-balance instead of steadying me and helping me maintain some balance. I was probably concentrating too much then. At that time, Judy asked me to exercise. I realized then that I do some of my best work when I am already a bit tired. Perhaps my muscles "fire" better and my movements are more fluid -- more controlled -- after I use them for a bit. Speech went well and horticultural therapy went well, too. We made cornmeal muffins with the corn that we had ground the week before and did a lot of chatting.

One night during that time, Jim and I talked on the way home from having dinner at my parents' house. I had been trying to talk to him for days but something was always getting in the way. I have to give Jim a lot of credit for even listening, since it was bathroom-oriented again. He did ask if it was about the loo. What I told him is this: "I know this makes no sense, but everything seems to lead up to my 'going to the loo.'" I became fixated on the loo as I had become fixated on so many things during my recovery. The brain is a strange thing. Some thoughts seem to linger in my head and it is difficult to forget them. Brain injury is very different in different people. My doctors said I developed obsessive/compulsive disorder.

Each time I go to the loo, then, and to this day, I "go" as much as I possibly can because I am not certain of the condition of the next "loo." Jim asked me, "Do we ever not find you a bathroom?" While it is true that the Americans with Disabilities Act guarantees that I will find a handicapped accessible toilet of some kind, I sometimes believe that it is quite obvious that whoever inspected the bathroom for compliance wasn't in need of an accessible room themselves. Many of them are not really accessible. With my lack of balance and lack of coordination, I was quite sure I would have trouble negotiating most facilities.

I had an appointment with the neuropsychologist about that time. It had been quite a while since I had seen her. I was hoping these sessions would help me to understand how to get back to "my life," especially since I split my time between two houses, living with Jim and with my parents. Even now, I sometimes feel like a tennis ball. It can become very confusing at times. I am so glad that I can be home, but it seems like things that I need -- the jeans or shoes that I want to wear, or the magazine that I want to read -- are generally at the "wrong" house; the other house.

I also talked to the doctor about how I was getting along with everyone and how that, too, made me feel pulled back and forth. I really felt like Mom and Jim "ganged up" on me one night. Perhaps I had it coming, but I don't know how I could have made things happen differently. They said I had been treating them like servants, asking them to get things for me when I could get them myself.

Perhaps I *had* been, without realizing it. I am so slow moving about and it's very cumbersome and difficult to move in my chair, but I guess that is not the question. If I wanted something, then I should have been the one to get it.

It seemed that, in some instances, they were pushing me away and wanting me to be more independent. In other instances, they felt that I needed to be protected and wanted me to remain close. I just wasn't able to figure out which was which! This is something we are still working out: when to let go and when to hold on. It would be helpful if we could find some balance. "Finding balance" truly has come to mean many things in my life.

Chapter 12
Milestones, Blessings and Challenges

After I went home, I remember thinking that I would go back to Wesley and volunteer in some capacity. I wanted to show my gratitude for the care that I had received. I thought that perhaps I could transport patients to therapy, or something. It didn't matter that I couldn't drive or that I couldn't even walk. Details were not important to me. I simply wanted to help and to say, "Thank you."

I suppose that shows in my mind, I still thought of myself as I was before my illness occurred. I am not too certain that is such a good thing. I place no limitations on myself, even though there are some. I think I can do everything, and I have to accept that I cannot.

Even housework has become a challenge. It is hard for Jim to keep up with his job and take care of our home, too, and I cannot do many things that used to be easy, so we hired someone to clean our house. It bothered me that we had to hire someone or ask Mom and my aunt to clean. I know we are really very lucky to have help, but Jim and I still wish we could do it ourselves.

Once, when our cleaning woman wasn't going to be available for several weeks, Mom and I went to Cambridge to catch up on the chores. We were there for about four hours and could have spent a lot more time.

Mom also did my laundry because, because from my chair, I cannot reach the buttons on the machines. Mom has told me that she wouldn't do the laundry if she really did not want to. I do fold the clean clothes, but still I feel so unproductive.

Moving breakable things to dust is impossible for me. I do not feel steady enough. With my ataxia, I never know what my hands will do. Sometimes they have a life of their own. Whenever I do something with breakables or with a knife, I stop and say to myself or out loud, "Where is the nearest doctor?" because in our little town there is no hospital. It is always good to know who can stitch me if necessary!

I sat in the kitchen one day with the vacuum cleaner and realized, to my extreme frustration, that it was simply too heavy and too cumbersome for me to push around.

Next, I tried to use a dust mop and that didn't work very well, either. I kept hitting myself in the back of the head with the handle. It was just too long. After I hit myself with the handle five or six times, Jim, being the good sport that he is, suggested we try cutting the broom handle off. That worked much better!

We keep trying new ways for me to adapt, and I am still trying to adjust to a different way of life. I am not able to work outside the home, and I have had to trade flipping bales of soilless mix up onto the greenhouse bench for using a computer keyboard. It has not been an easy adjustment for anyone.

Knowing how much gardening means to me, Jim raised some of our flower beds so that I could reach them more easily without having to bend over too far. Now, I can more safely climb out of my chair and work in the soil, but early on, this helped: bringing the plants up to me. Jim also installed a mini-greenhouse for me, so I can get an early start on seed sowing every year.

Even this -- part of my former career and one of my favorite activities -- has become difficult. My lack of organizational skills gets in the way. This is based, I believe, on my bad memory. I used to be a very organized person. My clients counted on me to think on my feet and quickly make decisions. Now, I cannot seem to focus.

Once, in trying to complete my own seed order for my summer garden, I had trouble weighing all the parameters that I used to measure without even thinking much. There were too many seed varieties to choose from, and I couldn't seem to remember different plant characteristics, such as height, how much sun versus shade each one required, or what specific colors I needed.

I worked on the order with Jim for a while and that helped, but when I continued by myself, I got confused again. Finally, Mom helped me finish. When someone works with me, I am better able to focus and attend to the job. On my own, I feel "swamped." I guess the give and take of collaborating keeps me on task and it stops me from second-guessing myself so much.

Having the love and support of my family has meant as much to my quality of life and recovery at home as it did when I was hospitalized. Anyone in my position understands this and would agree.

Even though we have our differences -- as do all families -- I appreciate how much my family does for me, and the years since I have been home have been full ones.

Almost every morning in Salem, friends and family members stop in for a coffee break. It is great to see everyone and to hear all the chatter about what is going on around town.

During our coffee club chats, I have learned a lot about the things that happened during the worst parts of my illness -- a time that I cannot remember. I was told that Mom's sister Carol and her husband Bob hosted Thanksgiving dinner from their motorhome when I was in the hospital in Syracuse. For some reason, Uncle Bob could at times, get a response from me when no one else could. He would raise his voice and say, "Megon, squeeze my hand," and I would. At the time, anyone else who visited me could tell I was "in there," but Uncle Bob was usually the only one I "answered." They all continued to visit me while I lived at Wesley.

All of my aunts and uncles visited me at one point or another during my illness and kept my parents company when I wasn't very responsive. In fact, I am told the administrator at Wesley used to say he "could tell when Meg has visitors, because the building tips on the side" where my room was located. I was lucky to have so much company then, and I am lucky to have that same company now.

My mother's brother, Uncle Kenny, and his wife, Aunt Rose Mary, quite often stop for a visit. Sometimes Uncle Ken will bring us a trout that he caught, and some good grilling follows. With or without trout, his visits are always entertaining. Having lived on the Battenkill River all his life, he is an accomplished fisherman. Of course, being a fisherman, he has great stories (often embellished, I'm sure) that I enjoy listening to. His adventures with his friend John are the source of humorous entertainment. It seems John prefers an Adirondack sunset and a glass of wine to doing any actual fishing.

My father's brother, Uncle Jack, and his wife Aunt Pat, are coffee regulars too. Aunt Pat and I often talk about our gardens and houseplants. My mother's sister, Aunt Barbara, and her husband, who is also named Jack, are part of the club. Barbara's Jack drove the ambulance when I moved between various hospitals and rehabs. When I "woke up" at Wesley, I do remember feeling like they were there visiting quite a lot. How thankful I am for their company and for the company they provided my parents. Uncle Jack used to get Jim out of the house on golf outings, but these days Jim doesn't get much time off. When he does take time to himself, he usually goes fishing where he can really be alone and get away from everything.

When I'm not having coffee with the gang, I usually spend my time in Salem doing exercises, reading, or working on the computer. My parents think I spend too much time on the computer, but it sometimes takes me longer to navigate it. I have also spent a lot of time writing this book and researching recipes or writing recipe indexes.

I love cookbooks, and one Christmas, as a present to my family and close friends, I put together a cookbook of family recipes, including some from my grandmother, who has passed away. I wanted everyone to have these recipes -- a little bit of our family history -- to hand down to future generations.

Sometimes, especially around the holiday season, I cook or bake with my mom. We have tried to find different ways of using a workspace, so I can do a lot of the preparation myself. Sometimes, I stand and lean against the counter; other times, we put the mixer on my tray, which attaches to the arms of my wheelchair.

Before we decided baby carrots really were better for him, I even delved into making dog biscuits for our dog, Jasper. All the canines in our extended family continue to benefit from this ritual as I still bake biscuits for eighteen "family dogs" on Christmas Eve. The peanut butter variety is an especially big hit. For a while, I also sold dog biscuits at a nearby garden center when a local author who writes books about dogs was there.

I don't do much baking at home because the stove is too hard for me to work with, and Jim's strength is in cooking, not baking. Gone are the college days when Jim's idea of preparing a gourmet meal consisted of putting a can of vegetable soup and a can of water into a pot, filling the can with raw quick-cooking rice to "measure" it, and then pouring it into the soup to cook it. Over the years, his kitchen skills have become decidedly more sophisticated and he's also become quite a grill master.

The grilling works out great, because Jim and I like to spend as much time outside as possible, at least in the warmer months. Keeping up with the vegetable garden, the flowers and regular lawn work takes up a lot of time, but we enjoy it. Well… Jim might say "enjoy" is a relative term …

Having only four days out of every eight at home together, we try to get as much done as possible.

A few years ago, Jim had to remove several old pine trees that were in very bad shape and hanging a little too close to the back of our house. In their place, he built a deck and gazebo that we call our "tree house" in honor of the trees that were removed. Adding a chiminea and some simple furnishings made it a perfect spot. It's a good place to serve dinner, and in the evenings we love to sit out there by the fire and chat or just spend time together in the quiet.

We had the great pleasure of hosting my brother Michael's wedding to Elizabeth. It was a lovely wedding and we were only too happy to provide the setting. The flowers in the yard and our little tree house added just the right touch to a wonderful day. I even danced -- with a little help from Jim and my cousin Mitch and his wife, Lisa.

During the winter months, we stick close to home, except during the holiday season. Since we don't have children, we tend to do the family visiting. Jim calls us "The Road Crew."

The December after my second re-awakening, we added an extra outing to our calendar -- Jim's company holiday party, which was held in Saratoga. Since it would be a late night, we planned to stay at the Gideon, a beautiful old hotel near the event.

Early every morning for days before the event, when I woke up I thought about that party. It would be the first time I attended something so elaborate in quite a while and I was kind of excited about it.

The night before the party, my mind was racing and I had difficulty falling asleep. It had suddenly occurred to me that Jim should ask for a "handicapped room," whatever that would be in an old hotel. I didn't think of myself as "handicapped." What did that word mean exactly, anyway? Jim said he didn't think of me as "handicapped" either.

I was also thinking about all the people we would see, the clothes that I would wear, and those that I would take with me for the following day. I finally went to sleep hoping that everything was under control.

The day we went, Mom packed my overnight bag instead of me. I didn't do a thing to get ready for that outing; I didn't even help. I used to keep track of a business, but I was not even trusted to remember everything for my overnight bag. Silly, but it was important to me.

I managed to shake off these feelings without much difficulty, and Jim and I ended up having a great time at the party. The band was superb. The food was unbelievable and abundant. The other guests were fun and Jim was the perfect date.

That night, I took my first drink of wine from a glass. It may not sound like much -- certainly not an important occurrence, but to me it was. I still shake so much when I concentrate too hard that I don't generally drink from a glass or even from a plastic cup, unless it has a top. I had taken straws and a plastic cup with me, just in case, but at the party I decided I wouldn't use them.

Jim held the stem of my glass in case I started shaking too much. It was of course red wine. He only let go when he saw I was handling it well, but his hand didn't move far away from the glass. It was good to know that I was capable, if not always consistent. This was another big deal for me -- a very positive one.

Two days later, Christmas day dawned snowy white. We had had twenty inches of snow! Because of the weather, our usual busy holiday proceeded at a much slower pace. We had breakfast at my parents' house, then went home and opened our gifts from each other. We had dinner at a regular time, instead of having it late or not at all, as we had done in other years when we were "on the road."

After Christmas, we visited my brother and his family in Rutland, Vermont, and had a great time. My niece Emma and her younger brother Sean were teenagers then, and I noticed so many changes in them. It bothers me that I missed so much of them growing up. When I first got sick, my parents told me that Emma used to crawl in bed with me and color pictures that she would leave for me. I still have some of them. Emma and Sean are both adults now. Sean and his wife just welcomed their first son, so I'm a great aunt. My niece and my nephew are now making lives of their own in different parts of the country, so I'm glad we had that year and a few other Christmases together.

The day after our trip to Rutland, we went to see Jim's family in Johnstown, NY. Visiting with them that year was especially nice, because it was the first time all five brothers and sisters had been together in years and the conversation was lively. It was fun to see them all together! The year before, Jim had gone to his sister's house by himself because I had been so sick.

When Jim has vacation, we sometimes take trips in our motorhome. Together with my parents, we have gone to Pennsylvania several times. Whenever we go, we visit the Amish markets to purchase all sorts of goods that we take home with us. Cheeses and breads and desserts, are some of our favorites.

Much of the market is open air, with several buildings containing many things, such as an old-fashioned butcher shop with display cases full of fresh and smoked meats and sausages waiting to be custom-cut; produce stands with mounds of fresh and delicious-looking fruits and vegetables; bakeries with their crusty bread, whoopee pies, shoofly pies and apple dumplings; and shops with handmade crafts where Jim found the wooden plaque that now decorates our front door.

Over the years we have taken a few other trips, as well. I remember being in Freeport, Maine, one really hot summer day. I didn't hear the remark at the time, but Jim told me later that a little girl pointed at me and told her mother that she wished she had a chair like that. I don't know exactly what the woman said, but I think the little girl received a lesson in "being careful what you wish for."

For a while, we traveled only in our motorhome, mostly for practical reasons, but also because I was afraid to fly. Even though my neurologist had told me my shunt would be fine, I had been concerned about how an airplane ride would affect it considering the frequent cabin pressure changes that occur during a flight. I never again wanted to experience a headache like the one that started my ordeal. This limited our range for a bit.

It was my brother Mike who finally convinced me to fly for the first time since my AVM. He encouraged me to go with my parents to Florida for a week. To my great relief, the shunt was fine on the plane, as predicted, but I had to experience it for myself.

I'm glad I did. We had a wonderful time visiting Sanibel and Captiva Islands, became reacquainted with some relatives living there, swam, ate quite a lot of grouper, found gorgeous seashells and saw some beautiful sunsets.

Another trip I have fond memories of is one we took to Nova Scotia to visit an old family friend Leo Burns and his wife Deb. Jim and I went out on their boat and found ourselves surrounded by a pod of twelve-to-eighteen foot pilot whales. Leo cut the engines and all we could hear was the sound of the whales blowing air out of their blow holes.

An almost unbearably hot day in June one year found us all (including Jasper, our dog) at my nephew Sean's graduation from Marine boot camp at Parris Island, South Carolina. Mike's son was about 19 at the time.

Jim and I cruised to Alaska the year we had been married for twenty-five years. We went alone and, with no additional help, everything went smoothly. Well, almost everything. Perhaps I should say nothing happened that wouldn't supply us with a good laugh in the future.

It was not easy on Jim: juggling tickets, luggage and me. It was not easy for me either. I played a different role in travelling, and I was having difficulty coping with it. I had to learn -- once again and quickly -- to let someone else take charge and make the important decisions.

As we disembarked in Seattle, I overheard a group of women comment on the fact that, even though I was in a wheelchair, I was still traveling and their friend could have come along. I am still "Megon."

It bothers me that most people view me differently now. I suppose that's natural. I am not even the same "independent Meg" that I was to my husband, and it upsets me that he's had to become acquainted with a different person, even if I don't feel so different -- certainly not the "vulnerable thing" that I should feel like.

Jim has had to do simple things for me -- like cutting my fingernails -- which I so badly wish I could do for myself. I try to remind myself that I wasn't even feeding myself when I first returned home and certainly required so much more "upkeep" then.

When you consider all the silly little things, like cutting my nails, it is rather a lot to expect of someone else. Perhaps that is why any time I relearn something -- or rather, retrain my body to do something, it is such a fulfilling experience.

After my AVM, I could not tie my shoes because my hands shook too much for me to be able to hang onto the laces, and I could not coordinate the steps involved. I could not remember the steps I had already take and those yet to come. Even a task this simple is really an intricate activity that we all take for granted. We learn to tie a bow when we are three or four and then with practice, it becomes automatic.

At Wesley, I was given "pegs" for my shoes. They were made of plastic and fit through the shoes' eyelets. A bow was always tied in the laces and the bow slipped over the peg, so it looked like my shoes really were tied.

I loved those pegs because they allowed me to appear just a little more "normal." At the same time, I hated them because of what they represented.

One day, I entered into my journal, "Today I finally tied my shoes! It has been seven long years, but I am still making progress and finding ways to overcome things that are difficult for me. I tied my shoes!" *I finally can tie my shoes.*

Epilogue

I wonder...will I blame things on my AVM forever? Was it because of the AVM that I was faced with health problems that summer, many years after the AVM interrupted my life? Or was it simply because it was an extremely hot day that might have had an effect on anyone? It was an unusually hot summer -- the hottest one on record, the meteorologists said.

On what would become the hottest recorded temperature for June twenty-second, I decided that it really was of utmost importance that I go outside and check my plants. I was on my way back to our house to find Jim and ask him if he could "lug" a hose for me. That really should have been a clue to me that something was wrong. I would never admit that I needed, that I wanted, help unless I tried and it proved to be something I was just not capable of doing.

It was there that Jim found me...in the drive on my way back to the house to find him. I was incoherent, slumped in my chair, and my right hand was twitching. Jim had to think quickly. He took me up on our porch where I would be in the shade, put cool water on my face, and dialed 9-1-1. Then he waited. They kept Jim on the phone answering questions about my condition and our location until an ambulance could arrive. After approximately five long minutes, an ambulance did arrive. The ambulance crew put more cool water on me and took me to a hospital in Bennington, Vermont, where I stayed for several hours being treated until it was suspected that I was having seizures and needed to see a neurologist.

At that very time, my blood pressure "crashed" and was 70 over 20. The closest available neurologist was in Albany, New York, and, because of my medical history, we needed to expedite my transfer. We flew there in a helicopter -- another flight I have no memory of -- and met a neurologist with whom I wasn't acquainted.

My parents came and spent that first day in Albany with me so Jim could go home and get some rest. I don't remember my parents being there, but I do remember the magazines they brought me to occupy my mind. I can remember carrying them with me.

I don't remember a great deal about my time in Albany. I do remember the pancakes that were served for breakfast on my second day there -- buckwheat -- something I had never sampled before (a good sign -- my appetite had returned!). I also remember that the head nurse on duty at the desk got quite perturbed, finally coming to my room to tell me she was tired of hearing my voice when I needed a bed pan in the night. I remember feeling angry and very confused at the time. Several hours later, I learned I was given five liters of saline to replenish my body fluids. No wonder I had to pee so much!

Also, I was in General Recovery, and I recall disliking to wake up and call for the bedpan because the woman in the next bed was so loud that it made getting back to sleep nearly impossible.

I stayed in the hospital Thursday through Saturday. I phoned my parents on the way home to let them know I had been discharged saving them a trip to Albany, which was about an hour away. At the same time, I requested a Delmonico steak!

I continue to practice standing and walking, but because of my lack of balance, I still rely on a wheelchair to get around. Despite doing eye exercises, I still have problems seeing and my ataxia affects my coordination. Consequently, trying to attend to ordinary things can take a bit longer now and leave me feeling very frustrated and angry. Even transferring things from one handbag to another can be a struggle when you are all thumbs and your vision is not good. I have to be reminded to be patient with myself.

Probably what bothers me the most is that I have so much trouble with my speech and some people cannot understand me. It can be difficult to convince them that it's "my fault" and can be affected by so many things, such as how well rested I am. I am fine in so many ways. I don't have headaches anymore and I truly do feel lucky to be alive, but I did think I would be much better by now. It certainly seems like I have "paid my dues."

Recently Jim and I were discussing my frustrations when he looked at me and said, "Megon, you had part of your brain removed, and you think you can walk away from that?" That really hit home. It made me stop and think, for a moment, about what has happened to me. I *know* that an AVM can even lead to death.

Over the years, Mom, Dad and Jim have become more receptive to talking about the past and that has been very helpful. When I was first trying to piece things together, I felt like they were shutting me out because I was asking too many questions. I am not sure I understood why everyone wanted to forget that time, and I felt incredibly isolated. It was hard to deal with all of my physical struggles without knowing or understanding what had happened to me, but I didn't feel I should ask them too much about my situation -- ask them to think about it yet again.

It was a big, uncomfortable step for Jim to share his journal with me; with him possibly having to "relive" some hellish events. I am, however, very grateful to him for sharing so much with me. It really is the way I learned of many things. Having a chronology of events has helped me to understand a great deal of what was, at times, a confusing situation for me.

Mom has been helpful, not only in telling me stories about who visited me and when, but also in sharing information she found about brain injury. I learned that when the blood supply to a small part of the brain is interrupted, the cells in that area die and the function controlled by that area is lost. Sometimes, another area of the brain will take over. I keep hoping that will happen and I will have my balance back, so I will be able to stand.

One of Dad's contributions has been our excursions out of the house. He takes me for walks on nice days or sits with me on the back porch at other times providing a much-needed rest for my mother and a welcome change of scenery for me.

One thing my arteriovenous malformation did supply me with was time. I had plenty of it on my hands and wanted to find something meaningful to do with it. My thoughts turned back to taking another step in my horticultural education: becoming a Master Gardener. This was something I wanted to do, and had *planned* to do, but when I was running my own business, I couldn't work the required classes into my schedule. After a certain point in my recovery, I felt able enough to try it and finding time was no longer an obstacle. So I took the course and finally became a Master Gardener.

The class met once each week for several weeks and was a chance for me to meet with people who enjoyed the same interests. Several lecturers, experts in their fields, taught us about their areas of specialization, providing information which we could pass on to any gardener who might ask us later.

I still attend horticultural therapy in Ballston, and have made good friendships there. I am very lucky that the program is available to me. It allows me to continue working in a horticultural environment, which I love. It is remarkable to me that, when I was a college student, I was participating in a horticultural therapy program in a retirement home near my apartment in Ithaca, New York. I used to plan gardening projects to foster the residents' interest in horticulture. Now I am in need of therapy myself.

When I first became ill, none of us had even heard the term "AVM." My parents and Jim, therefore, had to learn as much as they could even as they struggled to find help for me. I have never wanted or intended for this book to become a directory of doctors, rehabs or hospitals, although my family always said that they wished more resources had been available to them. They gathered information where they could.

One valuable source was a book written by a woman who had had an AVM. When I became able, I read it too, and I do think it helped me to understand a bit. Someone else had had an AVM, had survived it, and had rebuilt her life. Some of her experiences sounded familiar and her story gave me courage. I can only hope that my writing will do the same for someone else.

Telling my story has become a way to understand and process what has happened to me. Given my ongoing difficulties with my memory, it helps to have reminders of where I've been and how far I've come. I suppose I wrote to get things off my chest a bit, too. It does become quite bothersome when people cannot understand me -- when I can't make myself understood, especially with Mom and Jim, the two people with whom I spend the most time. Perhaps because I am most comfortable with them, I forget to "take a deep breath" and "speak in shorter sentences" so I don't run out of air: strategies that I learned in speech therapy at Wesley so long ago. When I speak, though, things sound fine in my own head, so I don't know how to fix them.

I wish, too, that my vision could be better. I have done various exercises prescribed by my neuro-ophthalmologist, but I still suffer from vision problems that can't be alleviated by corrective lenses. This *can* affect how well I understand what other people say, because my vision is only corrected to 20/60 and I still have some double vision. I think people read lips and faces and body language more than they realize when they communicate with each other. It also plays a part in my balance.

Trying to read and write has become very difficult, as well. Even watching television or a movie is challenging. It is so difficult to see and remember characters.

Having a home with Jim and being able to stay with my parents when Jim is working has given me the chance to live as normally as possible.

Yes, Jim is still in the picture. In our experience, with so much stress involved, such a situation tends to lead to separations. There are an awful lot of people that we met in rehabs who are all alone. It's been a long road, but Jim and I are still learning. We've come far, but we still have a long way to go.

When I was unresponsive, someone started an angel collection for me. I didn't remember it at all -- who started it, or that it was even started. My parents later told me that anyone coming to Wesley to visit me could look up at the building and pick out my room. It was the one with all the angels flying in the window.

At home one day, Jim brought something to show me. It was another angel I received at Wesley -- the one he had given to me -- and I definitely did remember her. A figurine with her arms folded across her chest, saying, "I love you," in sign language, displaying what I could only think at the time and could not say out loud to Jim or to my parents. Each night before they left the rehab, I made that sign for them. They are the real angels in my life. They have never given up on me. For that I am grateful.

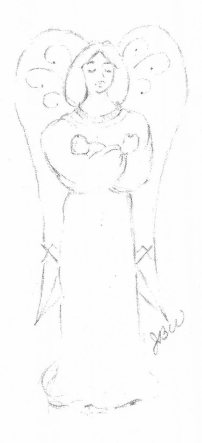

Appendix
Jim's Journal

The following pages contain Jim's journal, which is such an integral part of my story. Luckily, he kept it, allowing me to become acquainted with people and places I had no real knowledge of. It is fundamental to my story, yet still, it depresses me a bit to know it exists. It discusses so much that I was not aware of. I could not have been that ill and my family could not have been faced with such a difficult time.

<u>Jim's Journal</u>

Day 1: Sat. July 9

About mid-day Meg was in Ithaca with Linda when she got a headache. She took aspirin and it went away. Later, at about 5:30, she got a worse headache that became so painful that Linda took her to the hospital in Ithaca. When she arrived she was unconscious. They did a CAT scan and found a cerebral hemorrhage at the base of her head, which was creating serious pressure on the cerebellum and brain stem. She had to be transferred to Syracuse for emergency surgery. She arrived in Syracuse at 8:30 p.m. where she went to O.R. ASAP. We arrived at about 12 a.m. & she came out of O.R. about 12:15 a.m. We spoke with her neurosurgeons. It was grim. About the best they could say was Meg was a little better than when she arrived.

Day 2: Sun. 7/10

After 4 hours in the recovery room (it's now 4:30 A.M.), they wheeled her past us to I.C.U. They tried to prepare us for what we would see but I don't think that's possible. I was scared, as I have never been scared for someone else before. After an hour of getting her set up on machines and stabilizing her, they let us see her for a while. Nurse Pat introduced us to I.C.U. and began to explain what happened and what the machines are and how they work. Meg was unconscious, unresponsive, the vent was breathing for her. To see her this way was unbearable but she needed me. When I touched her, I felt something from her. It was like a subliminal message. She was glad I was there. She was reassuring me! She remained comatose all day and all Sunday night.

Day 3: Mon. 7/11

The vigil continues. I've been talking to her and stroking her arms and hands but there's nothing -- no movement, she's still riding the vent. About 9 a.m. she opened her eyes for me. The poor girl looked like a deer in headlights. But those were the most beautiful eyes I'd ever seen. A Miracle! Her neurosurgeon left O.R. to see for himself!! Meanwhile, her nurse had Meg hold up 2 fingers on her right hand and she did! The doctors told us the sooner she woke the better the prognosis. We were ecstatic. At this point, the doctors ordered a CT scan to check the damage. It wasn't real encouraging. She had blood and spinal fluid pooled in the ventricles.

Day 4: Tues. 7/12

When she greeted me Tuesday morning, she gave me a big grin and I was in heaven. The progress was much better than expected. The doctors say she's beating the odds! They've been weaning her off the vent and today about 8 a.m. they pulled the tube (extubated). She did a lot of coughing to keep her airway clear. She was working too hard and becoming exhausted just trying to breath. Her blood oxygen level dropped so they re-intubated her about 9 a.m. We were all very disappointed but Meg was most of all. She even pouted and wouldn't perform for the nurses until we called her bluff! I did this by just saying to her, "Meg, I know you're upset, but if you can understand and respond, we need to know that." We knew she was unhappy. Her eyes are still glassy and unfocussed but they seem a little more natural now. Her hand and foot movement is improving all the time -- her right is much better.

Day 5: Wed. 7/13

The progress continues. Today we brought in music and she tapped her feet (mostly right). She's moving both hands, feet, legs and arms -- the left is getting better but it takes much more coaxing. She loves the music. It's amazing how much of her sense of humor has shown through all along! On Tues. when asked if I was a pretty good nurse she gave the so-so hand gesture!

Day 6: Thurs. 7/14

We had a little scare this am. She had been performing real well all night but when the doctors came on rounds at 7 a.m., they couldn't wake her very easily or completely so they ordered a CAT scan to see if she had a re-bleed...back to reality!! It seemed to take forever. I finally heard she was okay. The ICP (intercranial pressure) was low. The scan was the same as Monday's. As it turns out, Meg "told" the nurse that she doesn't like one of her doctors (no-one does) and won't do anything for him. As he examined her he began to get in her face and yell "give me two fingers, Meg" and she responded with the middle two!! She had the whole ICU cracking up...nurses, interns and all! She's doing great. Her leg and arm movements are improving (left more slowly). Mike gave her her glasses and we showed her pictures of the puppies and her and Emma. She could see them and loved them. So far, she is amazing everyone. ATTA GIRL!

Day 7: Fri. 7/15

Meg is constantly getting better. Movements are more controlled and more exaggerated. They turned off the vent again and after about 2 hours, she was very sleepy -- wouldn't wake -- wouldn't move -- another scare. They put her back on vent and she responded well soon after that. Marcia arrived about 10:30 p.m.

Day 8: Sat. 7/16

Good day. Lots of visitors. Meg was getting a lot of exercise moving arms and legs. She can hold her butt off the bed now, change position, etc. She shows constant improvement. She's staying awake for longer periods now. She's going several hours -- didn't fall asleep until 10:30 p.m.

Day 9 Sun. 7/17

Slept most of night. Still quite tired from visits. Sat in chair for a while and she liked it, but stayed tired. Marcia had to leave and that depressed her some, too. We're learning some sign language to communicate. She still does well with work-outs.

Day 10 Mon. 7/18

Rough night...had to have morphine. Angiogram scheduled for 8:30 a.m. They explained the procedure and got my consent. Two hours later, it was over. They found the AVM with excellent quality pictures. Meg behaved! Now comes the hard questions and decisions -- operate or wait. It seems like there are risks on both sides...arsenic or cyanide? I have to dig deep for what's best for Meg. Operate and remove the AVM or take a chance and leave it there?

Day 11 Tues. 7/19

She seems a little more alert again. The doctors decided to extubate her again. She's doing better this time. She's coughing and swallowing with some success. However, her breathing is labored.

Day 12 Wed. 7/20

She's still on her own with breathing. She's coughing and swallowing. She seems more restless and anxious now (Progress)! Awareness level increasing. Went home at 1:00 p.m. to "pinching party". The chrysanthemums had to be pinched! There had to be 40 people!

Day 13 Thurs 7/21

She's getting quite physical and easily agitated. She's able to sit up and roll around. They had her standing up for a few steps today. She has to be restrained so she doesn't hurt herself at night. The breathing is still a question. We're suctioning her airway frequently (every 1/2 to 1 hr.). About 8:30 p.m. they ran a scope down her throat and found her vocal cords are still not functioning properly -- they can't close when she swallows... she aspirates. They are considering a tracheotomy. Possibly during Monday's operation.

Day 14: Fri 7/22

Still seems fidgety. Breathes better today. She wrote her first letters today to I.D. a plant for a nurse! Went for a "walk" today. Supported her weight pretty well but didn't have balance. Not a bad showing. Her neurosurgeon told her about Monday's operation. I think she understood and agreed it was best. I think she trusts her doctor. Thank God.

Day 15: Sat 7/23

A pretty quiet day. Not too much activity. Not much scheduled. They're letting her rest for the operation.

Day 16: Sun 7/24

Another quiet one. The doctors ordered a lumbar puncture (spinal tap) to determine ICP and fluid buildup. The doctors thought her responses were a little slower than normal. ICP Test showed normal...Meg is playing with doctors again. She got out of bed twice and walked around bed... exhausting for her.

Day 17: Mon. 7/25

She had another restless night. They think she has shifted to being p.m. active. Probably due to us calming her during the day -- She sleeps better with us around! We're now just waiting and sweating as the time nears for the surgery... scheduled for 3 p.m. ... It's 2:30 p.m. and she sleeps peacefully almost unaware of what's to come. She's incredibly strong and brave. I admire her for her courage. She's been so cooperative even though she's aware of the pain and discomfort. The throat suction is especially torturous for all of us, but she endures it without resistance. 6 p.m.: Her neurosurgeon told us the surgery was postponed due to another ahead of her. Unfortunately, it's been moved back 10 days!! They are still planning to do the trach and PEG tube.

Day 18: Tues 7/26

Signed papers for PEG tube tomorrow. She's a little depressed, I think. Not as active as she has been. I think she needs cheering and motivating. She sat in a chair most of the day. Also, did PT...seemed to help her spirits. She seems more aggressive and more easily agitated now. She sits up and swings her legs out of bed when uncomfortable.

Day 19: Wed 7/27

The day started out slow. Anticipating surgery for trach about 9:15 a.m. and PEG after. Well, as usual, pre-empted. I guess that means she's not bad enough to be a priority. So she went at 1:30 p.m. and returned at 5 p.m. She remained pretty tired rest of night -- occasionally restless or uncomfortable.

Day 20: Thurs 7/28

About 10:30 a.m., they put in the PEG (feeding) tube. Had to sedate her to do it. She stayed groggy quite a while. This afternoon, she was transferred out of I.C.U. to the floor... a bigger adjustment for us than her! She's not getting nearly the attention that she was getting before. I don't think they know Meg and her abilities...she had to be restrained to protect her!

Day 21: Fri. 7/29

Getting fed more regularly. Getting stronger. Went to PT and OT today. Walked 80 ft. (supported). Threw ball and caught with Gail. I went home to do business and house chores. She's getting strong and tough to handle when she's uncomfortable. Agitates more easily. Frustrated with no communication ability.

Day 22: Sat. 7/30

Meg looks great today. Lots of visitors cheered her up. She walked in the hall today, supported on both sides. Showed full range of emotion -- laughed, cried, even joked. I was working with her neck exercises and when she got tired, she strangled me!...enough with the neck!!!

Day 23: Sun. 7/31

More visitors and more walking. Ed and Gail left late afternoon and Barb and Jack returned. Meg walked full length of hall in a.m. and again in p.m. (about 100 ft. both times). Her color looks great...she even seems upbeat. Nights are restless... she gets restrained.

Day 24: Mon. 8/1

A.M. PT was very active. She walked and then did leg lifts. Then went to OT and slept! She still seems to be on a p.m. schedule and wants to sleep days. She still doesn't have great stamina but she gets stronger each day. Her balance and posture are also improving. Sat up unsupported for 20 minutes during OT.

Day 25: Tues. 8/2

A down day today -- she seems pretty tired out even though her roommates said she slept well. She did some arm exercises and did some writing in OT. Ed & Gail returned from Salem and Barb & Jack left. Talked to her doctor, to confirm surgery on Thurs. Also, her throat condition...he said it's still too soon to tell.

Day: Wed 8/3

Got stitches out from trach and had it replaced in a.m. Missed some PT/OT. Still, had a good, active day. Went to OT kitchen and put dishes in

& out of a cupboard. Took Meg outside for about 45 minutes at 4:30 p.m. She loved the sunshine and didn't want the wheelchair to stop.

Day 27: Thurs. Aug.4

Today is surgery. No PT and OT, but she went on time -- about 1:30 p.m. Now we wait and wait! I guess we were quite misinformed. She was on the operating table 10 ½ hrs. Her doctor and nurse looked totaled. The doctor said things went as expected -- had some trouble controlling bleeding which increased the time. She still had Recovery and CT scan to do, so we left, semi-relieved, about 1 a.m.

Day 28: Fri. Aug 5

Meg is still out of it this a.m. She does respond to voice commands (slowly). CT scan showed ventricular swelling and blood...had to add ventriculostomy line. She is breathing unassisted through trach. Hopefully, we'll see more rapid development this time. They tried to keep her quiet most of day except for checks.

Day 29: Sat. 8/6

She looks a little better today. Some swelling has gone down. She moves more easily and responds quicker. Still has pain and not too comfortable. Still, she is progressing as expected.

Day 30: Sun. 8/7

A better day overall. Swelling reduced. Eyes are nearly even now. Moves quite easily. Still has some pain. Kind of an up and down day. Alert and trying to talk at times. Moves extremities well. Busy day for Meg -- she handled it quite well. Lots of visitors.

Day 31: Mon.8/8

Making arrangements for rehab this a.m. Meg's still slow to respond and shows no enthusiasm. Still not accepting tube feed. Started an IV feed today to help.

Day 32: Tues. 8/9

Another slow, relatively uneventful day in ICU. She's not sleeping real well. Too much background noise. I think it's wearing her down. Started a feeding IV on Mon. about 8 p.m. She was moved out of ICU to floor. Gail and I left for rehab tours Tues. a.m. Looked at two places. Removed vent today.

Day 33: Wed. 8/10

Viewed Rutland Regional in Vermont. Starting to feed again...slowly.

Day 34: Thurs. 8/11

Doctors say maybe 1 more week here. Hopefully, the next hospital will be ready. Meg looks better today. Responds in OT. Still has day/night confusion.

Day 35: Fri. 8/12

Another quiet day -- still has days/nights reversed. Reluctant to perform in OT & PT. They don't push it since any rest is welcome now.

Day 36: Sat. 8/13

Not much news. Meg's getting a little stronger -- walking more easily to 100'. Nights are still restless. Probably sleeps better when we're here.

Day 37: Sun. 8/14

Heard of Meg's fall. She fell out of bed at 11:00 p.m. last evening. She's okay. No injuries, thank God. Made arrangements to stay over with her. Slept really well that night. I think this will help get her day/night back on track. She shows no side effects from the fall. Marcia visited today -- going home from Blue Mt (Rose's wedding). Good to see her. Meg was not real responsive much of time.

Day 38: Mon. 8/15

Meg slept real well with me here last night. Doctors say she's ready to leave. The next hospital isn't ready...lost her post-op notes so we wait and keep after the people. Meg's much more active today to the point of being somewhat agitated. May be reaction to Marcia leaving. Had her chest A-line removed. I'll be staying with her again tonight.

Day 39: Tues. 8/16

Not a good day. Meg's not responding much to people. She seems withdrawn. The good news is that she's been clinically accepted in the Vermont rehab. They say that they'll have a bed by Tues. Meg had a very tough, restless night...me too!

Day 40: Wed. 8/17

A little better today -- more responsive. Did well in PT & OT. Walked twice in evening with Ed and me. Still restless...gave her a new sedative. I'm still on nights. They also stopped oxygen tonight -- humid air only.

Day 41: Thurs. 8/18

Today was better. The roller coaster strikes again, though. In PT she used a wheeled walker while a therapist steadied her. OT was also good. Got word Meg will move on Mon. to Rutland. Did spinal tap today to check ICP and fluid. Color showed no unusual pressure and color was a little off due to a little blood in fluid...normal for two weeks post-op.

Day 42: Fri. 8/19

Meg had her throat checked with scope -- they said her vocal cords look much better...almost normal! Then they did barium swallow & she did great! Her larynx closed nearly all the way. Very little leakage which should improve with time. She also had a good PT. She used an unwheeled walker.

Day 43: Sat. Aug. 20

A very restless day followed by a pain in the neck night. Nurses are scarce and snotty. I'm wrestling non-stop with Meg and I'm exhausted. I've gotten no more than 4-5 hrs. sleep all week. I've had as much as I can stand and I'm getting nasty.

Day 44: Sun. Aug. 21

Meg's still agitated: squirming and wrestling with us. It's like watching an infant in a playpen full of broken glass. The tension of being on edge all the time is making us all crazy. Meg got heavy sedatives tonight and she's still fighting and fidgeting 2 hours later.

Day 45: Mon. Aug.22

Travel day! It's tough saying goodbye, but great things are ahead! The ride was surprisingly quiet. She slept most of the way and only occasionally moved to get comfortable! Once here, at the new rehab, I had to admit her and then started with information and questions. PT, OT, and speech people stopped. The physiatrist, Internal Med, and Primary nurses all stopped.

Day 46: Tues. 8/23

Meg had a pretty restless night -- new surroundings make her nervous? I stayed until 11 p.m...haven't slept since Sat a.m.

Meg had swallow test again this a.m. It went real well. They'll be starting chocolate pudding and ice cream soon. In a.m. PT, she went for a walk (with help).

Day 47 to Day 54: Aug. 24 to 31

Events are much slower now. The life-threatening medical stuff seems to be behind us. Our expectations seem a bit high right now. We thought or hoped she would show rapid initial progress once in rehab, but it's not happening. Meg is still agitated and restless. She requires 24 hr. watch. She's quite capable of hurting herself and the nursing staff can't handle her needs. So Ed and Gail take turns during the day shifts and I cover nights. Nights are absolute hell. You don't have the benefits of visitors and therapists to break up the monotony and you see Meg at her worst. She's either sleeping or agitated and lately she's been very restless. In a 12 hour shift she sleeps about 4 hours.

I'm incredibly lonely. There's no one to talk to. No one to get things off my chest to. I feel so trapped and alone.

As for Meg's progress...it's hard to say. I don't see the therapy sessions and get only sketchy reports. They tell me things are improving...she's walking a little better; she's working on ADL's and is quite good at dressing and brushing her teeth. She has had a few spoons of food this week, including chocolate pudding.

Today, however, was a special day (Aug. 31). They blocked her trach for 1 hr. & the oximetry was great (97%). During that time they also had her try to talk. What were her first words? "Hi Mom," of course.

Tomorrow, we're having our first family meeting. I should have a better idea of where we are and where we're going after that.

Day 55-61: Sept.1 to Sept. 7

This has been a much more productive week. All members of the staff are encouraged with Meg's progress. She has been walking much better (still supported) and has much more control with her right leg. Her right arm is still quite weak. She favors the left. Her speech is still pretty weak and has to be drawn out of her. She doesn't speak conversationally; she counts, recites months, weekdays etc. and ID's pictures. Her attention span is a little better, but her medication is not working well yet. She still has a urinary infection and has to be straight catheterized every 4 hrs. She is still tube feeding, although she has had some pudding. They have been increasing the time her trach is plugged to where they are now up to 12-14 hrs. per day. Today (Sept. 7) they did a barium swallow and it turned out great. They should be removing her trach soon.

Day 64: Sat., Sept. 10

Pulled the trach today. Speaking and swallowing should come easier now or at least once it heals over. She had a very good day. Responding very well. Very alert. Saying a few words. Unsolicited hugs. Walking with support outside.

Day 65: Sun. Sept. 11

Meg did a 180 today. The head hangs, slow to respond. Unwilling to do much and the agitation level has increased. We wonder if pulling the trach had something to do with it, but the oximetry says not.

Day 66-68: Mon.-Wed. Sept. 12-14

The backslide trend is continuing and worsening. The therapists are noticing a dramatic change in her ability to focus, concentrate, and agitation is increasing. Doctors are puzzled. Her neurologist ordered a CAT scan. They believe it shows dilated ventricles, but they want to compare to Syracuse x-rays.

Day 70: Fri. Sept. 16

She continues to get worse as week "wears" on. The x-rays came from Syracuse and her neurosurgeon concludes this change is excessive fluid. Not life-threatening, but surely impeding progress. Drained it with a syringe and within hours there was a difference.

Day 74: Tues. 9/20

Over the weekend she continued to decline, becoming totally unresponsive by Sunday. She was conscious, but that's about all. Eyes dilated, little controlled movement, no reaction to stimulus. The doctors are trying to schedule a shunt ASAP and she's getting one today at 1 p.m. I took the day off to be here, and at 2:45 (slight OR delay) she went down to OR. They started at 3 p.m. Her neurosurgeon informed me that all went well at 4:20 p.m.! At 5:30 p.m. she was able to leave recovery and return to the room. Even though groggy, she was still agitated. A nurse gave her Tylenol w/codeine and within 15 min. she was asleep! The noticeable swelling on the back of her head was gone, eye movement seemed apparent with no dilation. It looks good. I pray this is THE turning point.

Day 75-83: Sept. 21-28

Right after the shunt, Meg's eyes seemed to clear some and the swelling went way down. However, the agitation was back, big time. That first day she squirmed and fought for 7 hrs. straight plus she had nausea and vomiting toward the end of the week. Agitation, nausea, unresponsive to therapy.

Her doctor said the release of pressure can be as disruptive as the build-up and only time will let her regain equilibrium. In the meantime, the discharge planner is saying a move to a different facility may be necessary since she isn't showing sufficient progress to keep insurance people happy. I guess there are legal definitions of acute vs. long-term and Meg's progress is long-term.

Day 84-95: Sept. 29-Oct. 9

It almost seemed like Meg was listening and after the "family meeting from hell," Meg is responding. She seems to be much more willing to work in therapy and interacts with visitors, follows motion, squeezes hands and we get pretty good thumbs up. She is not talking and we've noticed some spasms in the neck area.

Day 96: Oct 10th

As predicted, we had to relocate. The choices didn't leave much. Boston, New Jersey, Cortland and Niskayuna, New York. Jack made arrangements with Salem Rescue Squad to take Meg to Hilltop in Niskayuna. When we arrived, it was sheer chaos. A damn zoo. I felt pretty sick and sad to think that Meg had to spend time here. It was just not as I remembered it. I processed in quickly with a case manager. However, that's all that happened fast. It wasn't until 3 p.m. that a doctor saw her and nobody could do anything until then. So, no feeding or catheterization for almost 12 hrs. Therapists didn't show and the bed was a tiny, pathetic thing that she was beating herself up in. Slowly things began to happen. They set up a private room with mattresses on the floor and gave her food and resumed meds. They finally realized she is a danger to herself and got a one-on-one to stay with her through the night.

Day 97: Oct. 11

Today I arrived at about 9 a.m. and Meg was dressed, in a chair and in front of the nurse's station, ready to go. She was scheduled for therapy at 9:30 a.m. No show. At 11:00 a.m. no show again. I was ticked!! So -- back to Karen and got things straight. She finally got her wheelchair at 3 p.m. and we went outside for about an hour. The nursing issues are resolved; now let's get the therapy going. Her doctor ordered a 1-on-1 for 3 p.m. to 11:00 p.m. and 11 p.m. to 7:00 a.m. shifts so maybe we can rest easier at night.

Day 98: Oct. 12

Went to work today, but told Karen to call about therapy sessions. She did and it sounded good. Meg seems alert and responsive and seems to be accepting the move quite well. I arrived about 7 p.m. and she had a grand mal seizure. She stiffened up and stopped breathing in my arms. I can't believe how calm I stayed even though panic seemed to set in with the sitter. They gave her oxygen and suction at first then medication. After a couple hours, she fell asleep so I left.

Day 99: Oct. 13

Up at 4:00 a.m. and off to work. Called at 8:30 a.m. and found out she had a second seizure at 3 a.m. No calls, no word, and worse yet no doctor saw her until 9 a.m. -- 6 hrs. later. They decided to send her to the hospital for CAT, blood tests, chest X-ray and lumbar puncture. CAT looked normal -- no swelling, no bleeding. They sampled shunt instead of doing a spinal tap. Results showed no infection, thank God. We finally got a neurologist to admit Meg at 8 p.m. What a fiasco -- 12 hrs. in ER and nobody was doing anything or taking responsibility. We are lost, confused and no one is telling us a damn thing.

The feeding schedule is suspended. They put in a Foley catheter. There is swelling in the back of the head again and no explanation. The CAT scan shows ventricles are normal.

Day 100: Oct. 14

Arrived at 9:45 a.m. They were in the process of doing an EEG. She had a quiet night -- no seizures. Got no word on results of EEG but her neurosurgeon said swelling is quite normal. Not much happened today except Meg is still totally unresponsive and there are no answers.

Day 101: Oct. 15

Her doctor called and expressed concern with Meg's inactivity. I arrived at hospital at 11:45 a.m. Meg was sleeping. Her neurosurgeon checked in and was concerned for prolonged lethargy. Ordered a follow-up CAT scan. After comparing with Thursday's scan, he agreed that hydrocephalus was back!! Probably the shunt is plugged. He said they will monitor ICP ventricular pressure and possibly modify the shunt.

Day 102-107: Oct. 16-21

Meg's condition hasn't changed. She has steady vital signs and is breathing on her own, but she remains very inactive, moving her arms and legs very seldom. She moves her eyes well and seems to follow movements and the eyes look very natural. Her neurosurgeon seems to think she's in a resting period since there doesn't seem to be a medical reason for her lethargy.

10/27

Meg was returned to the rehab.

12/5

Up to this point, the progress has been slow. Starting from zero strength but good eye contact and movement. She gradually built strength and responsiveness over the weekend (12/3-4). We noticed the breathing, bloodshot eyes, and sleepiness. On Mon. a.m. she vomited and ran a super high blood pressure (210/145). They sent her to the hospital for tests and observation at 4 p.m. About 5:30 p.m. she had a seizure. (Naturally, no doctor to be found)! Did chest x-ray, CAT scan, and blood tests. Her temperature is also elevated

(101.5). Tests show nothing, except, of course, elevated white blood count. Urinary infection is back?

12/6

Had restful night on medications. About 9 a.m. had another seizure -- moved her to ICU, more medication but still labored breathing. Had to intubate her. Now on vent due to heavy sedation.

The neurosurgeon said there's no apparent shunt failure or infection. She may have scar tissue in esophagus from trach inhibiting breathing. There's still no explanation for the seizures. May be building tolerance to her medication so started a different medicine.

12/7

Stayed on ventilator all day. No response to commands. Eyes react to light. Her tongue protrudes. ENT waiting for stability. About 7:45 p.m. she opened her eyes briefly and breathed on her own a short time.

12/8

Had eyes open again. Her GP said she may have tongue muscle damage due to seizure and narrowing of airway. May have to re-trach. ENT is looking into it. Did EEG -- apparently inconclusive. She's slowly becoming more aware, keeping eyes open for longer and more frequent periods.

12/ 9

Meg seems a little more alert to people. Opens eyes on command. Eyes a bit wider than normal and do not follow movement. Still on ventilator -- relying on it most of the time. Going to do another EEG. This time using a drug that paralyzes muscles (Curare derivative) to determine what is brain and what is muscle spasm. She has to be on ventilator for this since it will stop voluntary respiration.

12/10

Our dog threw up all night last night. Not much sleep. Got to hospital about 12:30 p.m. Meg is not good. Fighting and coughing on ventilator -- taking rapid, shallow breaths -- up to 40/min.

Running fever of 102. Having muscle tremors (rigors) all over her body. Did EEG -- said it was not seizure activity. Also, blood in mouth may have been there from biting tongue and lip. Tongue still protrudes. Heart rate also still elevated at times to 138-140. BP is 154/94 at 12:30 p.m.; 122/82 at 1:00p.m. At 1:15 p.m., her temp was 106. Packed her with ice, started antibiotics. Took chest x-rays. 3 p.m. -- breathing more normally. Heart rate slowed somewhat to about 118 right now, and BP is 129/68. Seems to be resting more comfortably. Eyes open to voice and look natural. 3:25 p.m. BP 103/64. X-ray showed pneumonia on right side.

12/11

Murphy went to Vets today -- has intestinal obstruction -- may need surgery tomorrow. Meg seems to be holding her own. Her temp has stayed down but she's tired and sleeping most of the time, opening her eyes very briefly. She is riding ventilator and her tongue still protrudes although not as much as yesterday. She seems to respond to touch -- squeezing hands. Heart rate and BP have been pretty normal all day -- still on medication for BP.

12/12

Murphy had surgery about 9:30 a.m. to remove the stone from her digestive tract. Got to hospital 12:15 p.m. to find Meg in isolation. She contracted MSRA -- a staph infection (probably from Rehab) that is being treated with medicine. She's awake but not very responsive -- still very tired.

Still on vent and pretty much relying on it. BP and heart rate look good -- 114\74 and about 100 bpm. Tongue still swollen and protruding.

Temperature has been staying down. Had to start a new I.V. line and Meg responded a little to the pain. Tube feeding resumed last night and continues today.

12/13

Still having problems with feeding. Have isolated the staph infection -- MRSA (Methosilac Resistant Staph Auers) -- mask and gown, feeding with Pedialite. Started medication for MRSA. Vitals are stable. Still has pneumonia, UTI and MRSA. Riding vent.

12/14

Little change in overall condition. Vitals are stable -- temp. stays down. Riding vent but does initiate breathing occasionally. Still has infections. Eyes look little more natural and may be focusing on sounds or motions.

12/16

Progress is slow to non-existent. Her eyes do not level and focus. She's on the ventilator -- relying on it totally most of the time. About 7 p.m. she had a CT scan. Talked to her neurologist, but he had little information -- said EEG was normal. Drugs are controlling seizure activity well. Unable to explain lethargy and inability to initiate breathing. CT may show more. Still has UTI, slight pneumonia and MSRA.

12/17

Relatively quiet day. Stayed awake a little more and eyes looked better. Followed movement and sound with eyes on occasion. Still relying heavily on ventilator, but general appearance is better. Vitals are stable, still has infections, no drug change.

12/18

Awake most of day. Eyes look good. Follow sound and movement occasionally. Seems more alert. When awake initiates breathing some. Vitals -- good. No drug change.

12/19

CT. of 12/16 showed some improvement. Ventricles are smaller -- no bleeding. Vitals still good. Still relies on ventilator. Eyes look good and follow movement. Waiting on trach until MSRA clears up. Running cultures today.

12/20

Not much change. Still on ventilator full time -- some initiated. Eyes are better. Move naturally and follow motion better. Vitals are stable. Occasional gripping with both hands. Meds. are the same.

12/21

Infection cultures indicate she is free of MRSA. They have scheduled trach for 11:45 a.m. tomorrow. Not much change in general condition.

Still almost 100% ventilation. Eyes look good --
follow movement. Little or no physical movement.

12/22

Not much change. Went to OR for trach at 11:50
a.m. Still relies on ventilator had to be bagged for
transport. Trach went well. She was back in room
by 1:00 p.m. -- and awake! Anesthesia didn't
seem to linger. Stopped feeding until evening.
Saw marked improvement in eyes and in arm
movement.

12/23

Looks good today -- better color, eye contact and
movement. Still on ventilator but she breathes on
her own and ventilator assists. Infections are clear
(except UTI). BP and temperature remain good.

12/24

Meg continues to show improvement in general.
Eyes look good. She seems to keep tongue in mouth
most of the time now. Temp and BP remain stable.
Brought a boom box with Christmas music. She
seemed to relax to it and went to sleep. Ed & Gail

went to the family Christmas party at Carol and Bob's. Murphy went home with Mike.

12/25

Brought Meg gift from Dwyers...Raven/Murphy stuffed dogs. Cute. Meg has good color, good eye contact and movement. Temp., BP -- good. Still initiating breathing with ventilator in assist. She seems to be doing more of the work. Getting better.

12/26

Meg's having problems. Spiked a temp. of 103 at 12:30 p.m. Doing culture to see if infections are back. They'll do a chest x-ray for pneumonia. Very pale and exhausted. Started antibiotic. Seems to be breathing faster. Up to 18/min. BP is low -- 96/52. Shortly after she started one medication, she seemed to get better color and was more comfortable. Her eyes were not as good today.

12/27

Pulled A-line and Foley today. Respiration is much better -- ventilator is now at 2.0 and she runs 12-16 min., even when sleeping. Low-grade fever this am -- 101. Chest x-ray-clear. No results from other cultures yet. Coloring much better today.

12/28

Progress is slow but positive. Ventilator set on C-PAP (Continuous Positive Airway Pressure) -- which means she is initiating all her breathing and doing well. Urinating on her own without Foley catheter. Mouth and tongue area look better. Sleeps much of time now. Eye contact and movement not as good as it was before seizure, but getting better.

12/29

She came off the ventilator today -- doing well. Oxygen level is very good. Breathing pattern somewhat erratic.

1/3

Transfer day to Dartmouth. As usual, problems from the start. Meg's MRSA is back. The new rehab said it was "OK. " Ambulance team shows at 11 a.m., but not qualified to deep suction trach. No one at hospital is available, so we wait. Finally at 3:40 p.m., we got underway. Arrive at 7:10 p.m. All is in order and she's in her room by 7:15 p.m. Mike is here and waiting. At 9:30 p.m., doctors arrived, examined Meg and had already read her charts! Incredible!

1/4

Met the neurologist at 8 a.m. and got initial impression of team. It sounds encouraging. Could be possible shunt problems to be repaired or a 2nd shunt could be added to relieve pressure on back of head. Lots of tests today. EEG, EKG, MRI, CT, X-Rays. No conclusions at this point. Should have better idea after conferences with doctors. Established "home" at Motor Lodge.

1/5

Planning angiogram today...may have residual AVM. Meg's condition hasn't changed much -- not very responsive -- eyes bob and dart. She's not tracking. Respiration is improving and cough is getting stronger. Had angiogram at 11:15 a.m. and didn't return to room until 2 p.m.! Got word of results at 5:30 p.m. Said no sign of residual AVM. Recommending shunt revision. May be scheduled early next week. Haven't spoken to neurosurgeon yet. No sign of UTI but MRSA results are inconclusive.

1/7

Getting more responsive eye movements and tracking. Wiggled toes for P.T. Planning shunt revision next Tuesday.

1/8

Not much change in condition. More arm and leg movement, eyes look a little better. Infections are apparently under control. Her vitals are stable and respiration is normal -- good oxygen rate.

1/10

Did shunt revision this a.m. All went well. They had to replace entire length. No pressure with old one. When new one was placed, fluid came out under pressure! Sounds like right move. Slept most of day, but eyes look better and more movement with legs and right arm.

1/11

Arrived in a.m. from work -- went to bed. Saw Meg in late afternoon. Seems to be doing a little better.

More alert than she has been. Eye movements are quite good. A lot of swelling around right eye. They said it's due to surgery. Moving legs and right arm frequently now.

1/13

Meg continues to improve a little each day. Eye movement is quite rapid now -- not always fixed. Some degree of cross eyes. Moves right arm and both legs frequently now...stretching and repositioning. Right arm up on command -- seems more responsive in chair. Went with Mike to a rehab near Boston today. Not too impressed. Will look at another next week.

1/14

Wow. Came in today and Meg is in "full motion." Both arms and both legs are moving. She didn't seem agitated, just restless! She looked quite alert with good eye contact (this while in bed). Then got up in chair and fell asleep! Haven't been able to catch up with doctors in a while with road trip, etc. Hope to get updated on scans, tests and observations today.

1/15-24

Meg's condition hasn't changed much during this time. Various scans and tests have been performed and the conclusion is that she does not have any seizure activity at this time. Most of her involuntary movements are neurologically related as "pathway misfires" or incomplete neuro messages. Neurosurgeon has been monitoring pressure and swelling and CT scans are questionable at this time. There are no behavioral symptoms to indicate shunt failure, but he's not totally comfortable. Earlier this week her neurologist tried a couple drugs to enhance neuroresponse. They had very little effect -- so were stopped. Infections are under control and vitals are good.

1/20

Visited The Greenery in Massachusetts with Mike. My feelings were quite ambivalent. These places are all starting to look alike...Promise great things.

1/25

The neurosurgeon reconsidered CT scan and decided to do another shunt revision this p.m. Surgery lasted about 1-1/2 hours and went well. He said when he put in new shunt only a small amount of fluid came out so he inserted it a little deeper and relieved quite a bit of pressure. He seemed quite optimistic about Meg's prognosis and said areas affected were not critical and he has seen worse cases turn out well. Meanwhile, discharge planner is hard pressing for transfer. I insist no earlier than Monday.

1/27

Nausea continues (started yesterday) -- discontinued her feeding and started I.V. of potassium chloride to avoid dehydration. Breathing is somewhat labored, but she is alert, moves extremities well and tracks with eyes well...Glad she didn't transfer today as was previously planned.

1/28 & 29

Vomiting seems to be over and Meg looks good when awake. Seems alert and moving around more -- tracks real well and eyes look natural.

Not much else is new. Doctors haven't been around much this weekend. Move is still on for tomorrow. Not much looking forward to it. Hate to have to re-establish a "home base" -- especially in a major city.

1/30

Relocated to The Greenery in Boston. Staying with Heidi and Peter until we find an apartment. Not easy, not cheap.

2/1

Progress is very slow now. Meg is weak and responsiveness and movements are very slow.

2/14

Meg's trach was downsized ...seemed to go well... her oxygen saturation remains good.

3/8-15

Scheduled CT scan. Went well with minimal trauma. The scan was sent to her neurosurgeon and her doctors were all very pleased with shunt. Meg is steadily, albeit slowly, getting stronger and more alert.

3/16

Replaced Meg's trach today -- didn't downsize, just replaced. Meg's getting very lethargic again. Unresponsive and sleeps much of time. A check of her seizure medication level was very high. Adjusted level and Meg showed improvement rapidly.

3/17-31

Meg's progress is steady and slow. No major medical setbacks. Still has UTI, which is periodically treated with antibiotics. Celebrated Meg's 35th.

4/8

Meg's running relatively high blood pressure. May be upset with being wet and not changed or reacting to parents being upset.

4/11 to 5/30

Meg was showing some improvement early in this period. Deliberate movement, particularly with hands and arms, was improving. She was also in PT standing class on tilt board...holding head up and moving arms on request. Her seizure medication level has stabilized. Weather is getting good. We're outside as much as possible. As of about May 1, we started to notice a decline in alertness and activity level. This decline is steadily increasing.

5/19

Meg had CAT scan to investigate current condition.

5/22

Rehab neurologist reviewed scan with me and thought shunt was working too well! Producing "slit-like" ventricles. Sent scan to her first neurosurgeon. It was not received until 5/26 -- holiday weekend. Got answer on 5/30. They feel the shunt is working fine and don't mess with it. Should check into blood levels of various elements i.e. Dilantin, electrolytes, and ammonia. Results indicate all blood levels are in normal range!

5/23

Switching to valproic acid from Dilantin -- should be less sedating.

6/2

Made arrangements to transfer to Wesley Health Care and Rehabilitation Center in Saratoga Springs, New York.

6/5

Transferred to Saratoga. Was going to use Salem Rescue Squad Ambulance, but 4 a.m. that morning while transferring a patient to Albany Med, they hit a deer. Scrambled to get alternate...Cambridge Rescue loaned Jack theirs. Transfer went well -- no problems. This place is great -- well-run and organized. Some problem with trach -- not same brand and no replacement inner cannula.

6/6

When I got here at 10 a.m., Meg was up, bathed, and in a fitted chair! Wow -- fast! Some question about trach...brought in respiration tech to get it straightened out. Also PT and OT saw Meg a short time. In p.m., spoke with Speech and Social Worker for background and medical history. I'm very impressed with care, attitude and efficiency.

6/11

Meg ran temp of 104 today. Not sure what caused it. Doing blood, urine tests.

6/12

Tests came back. UTI -- not bad. Noted elevated white blood count. Did chest x-ray and found pneumonia. Started a new drug -- will continue for 10 days. Infection knocking her down, but still has good periods. Tracking well and using "yes-no" board.

6/21

Meg had follow-up x-ray yesterday...pneumonia has cleared up. Had trach replaced today. I think it was rougher on the nurses than Meg. She seems quite alert and there's minimal blood in sputum. Therapy is going well. Tracking and using "yes/no" board real well. Moving legs on command a small amount. Arms not doing much except during cough.

This was Jim's last journal entry. He was finally sure of my surroundings and that I would be well taken care of there. I would not be at all aware of my surroundings until sometime later. It had been a long road, but Jim and my parents could finally leave at night and be sure to find me in good spirits and in good physical condition the following morning. They were not always so sure of my well-being in the past.

Time Line

Ithaca July 6-July 9

Syracuse July 9-August 22

Rutland August 22-October 10

Hilltop October 10-December 5

Ellis Hospital December 5-January 3

Dartmouth January 3-January 30

Greenery January 30-June 5

Wesley June 5-September 4 (15 months)

Home September 4

Afterward

My stroke was a hemorrhagic stroke, meaning in my case, an AVM (arteriovenous malformation) -- or abnormally formed blood vessels -- burst, releasing blood into the surrounding tissue in my brain. Hemorrhagic strokes (bleeds) account for only about 13 per cent of stroke cases as opposed to ischemic strokes, during which a clot becomes lodged in a blood vessel leading to the brain.[3] With a hemorrhagic stroke, it is important only to get to a doctor as soon as possible. Damage has, in all probability, already taken place, as the pressure from pooling blood on the brain, has already occurred.

I could not know if what I was experiencing was an indication that my job was taxing, or that I was having a stroke. The pain I was experiencing in my neck could have come from any number

---

[3] http://www.strokeassociation.org/STROKEORG/AboutStroke/Typesofstroke/Hemorrhagic-Strokes-Bleeds

of things including the strain of flipping large bales of soilless mix up onto the potting bench in my greenhouse. The headaches could have come from the stress involved with running a business, such as late nights of number-crunching. It also would be impossible to distinguish between a hemorrhagic stroke and an ischemic one without having a CT scan or an MRI. During an ischemic stroke, a blood clot becomes lodged in a vessel supplying food and oxygen to the brain.

The three hour rule, meaning no more than three hours should elapse between the time the first symptoms of a stroke are noted and the time when medical help is received, applies only to ischemic strokes. With this type of stroke, medicines that are "clot busters" can be given to allow blood to pass through and to minimize the damage to the brain.

So much more information has become available to us since the American Stroke Association was founded, that quite a bit has already changed. For the most part, we are much more knowledgeable about strokes now. Although some things have remained the same, other pieces of information have been forgotten, as was evidenced by a group of Master Gardeners (myself included) that took a water break in the garden we all weeded one very hot day in June. None of us could remember the acronym "FAST[4]," which would allow us to recognize a stroke and act quickly to get help. One of the gardeners said that they devote a class to strokes now and she didn't understand before meeting me what a stroke had to do with "growing flowers."

I think the symptoms of a stroke are something we should all be familiar with.

The acronym we must all remember to help us recognize a stroke is as follows:

F-Face Drooping. Ask the person to smile. Look to see if the mouth is uneven.

A-Arms. Ask the person to raise both arms. Does one of the arms drift down below the other? Is one arm numb?

S-Speech difficulty. Have the person repeat a simple sentence, like "Water is wet." Do they repeat it correctly? Is the speech slurred? Is the person difficult to understand?

T-Time to call 9-1-1. If the person shows any of the symptoms, even if they go away, call 9-1-1 right away. It is now commonly known that there are three hours between the onset of a stroke and

[4] http://www.strokeassociation.org/STROKEORG/WarningSigns/Stroke-Warning-Signs-and-Symptoms

treatment for a stroke, before lasting damage is incurred.

It would be my goal to ensure that more people are aware of those easily remembered stroke symptoms along with the acronym "FAST."

Presently:

-someone in America has a stroke every 40 seconds[5]

--about 795,000 Americans have a stroke each year[6]

-Stroke kills about 129,000 people each year[7]

-on average, someone dies from a stroke every 4 minutes[8]

-stroke is the fifth leading cause of death[9]

[5, 6, 7, 8, 9] http://www.strokeassociation.org/STROKEORG/
AboutStroke/Impact-of-Stroke-Stroke-Statistics

Printed in the United States
By Bookmasters